What Every Great Teacher Knows

Practical Principles for Effective Teaching

Richard A. Gibboney
With Clark D. Webb

What Every Great Teacher Knows

Practical Principles for Effective Teaching

Richard A. Gibboney
With Clark D. Webb

Holistic Education Press
Brandon, VT 05733-0328

1-800-639-4122

http://www.sover.net/~holistic
holistic@sover.net

ACKNOWLEDGEMENTS

The authors gratefully acknowledge the many educators who have contributed their stories to this book. They are all Great Teachers in every sense of the phrase.

They also thank *The Active Learner: A Foxfire Journal for Teachers* for its permission to reprint "Offering Challenges..." (p. 33) and "Seven Years in a Foxfire Classroom..." (p. 93).

WHAT EVERY GREAT TEACHER KNOWS

Table of Contents

Part One

Introduction

Part Two

Eighteen Teaching Principles
With Illustrative Stories

Thinking and Experience

To my granddaughter
Megan Elizabeth Carr
Whose eagerness to learn
Reminds me daily of
What many of us
Have lost.

— R. G.
Birchrunville, PA
April 1998

Part One

Introduction

Introduction

It is essential that you read Part 1; Part 1 tells why *What Every Great Teacher Knows* was written and how you and your colleagues might use the powerful ideas in the 18 principles. The principles provide a framework of ideas which gives the wonderful stories told by teachers intellectual power. The "teacher knowledge" in the stories is a beautiful and too often overlooked complement to academic knowledge. Each kind of knowing is necessary and enriched by the other.

We know that you are busy and more than a little tired. Good teachers often feel this way. We also know that you are "fed up to here" with schemes marketed as "quick fixes" for whatever ails you educationally — schemes that promote the "easy implementation" of supposedly failure-proof programs more than the imaginative efforts of intelligent teachers.

We share these concerns. We believe deeply in the role that teachers play in our society. We believe that teachers and principals have had too little opportunity to share ideas about issues affecting the quality of learning with others at the school level. Too often talk about learning and teaching is lost in the welter of routine meetings; predictable, narrowly-focused staff development sessions; outside speakers with jokes; and the near-frantic worry about test scores — all of which de-emphasize the importance of learning and teaching and informed conversation with colleagues.

WHY THIS BOOK WAS WRITTEN

What Every Great Teacher Knows was written to help preserve and inservice teachers in two ways.

1. To provide a framework of ideas and values within which teachers could think about and discuss the ambiguities, problems, and satisfactions in teaching. We wanted to write a book about teaching that avoided

the shallow how-to technique trap that degrades the office of teacher (see Barth 1990; Gibboney 1994; Goodlad 1984; and Little 1982).

We wanted to write a book that assumed the intelligence of preservice and inservice teachers. We wanted to write a book structured by ideas (the principles) whose content (the teachers' stories) might encourage teachers to talk among themselves about the ideas and practices in their school. *What Every Great Teacher Knows*, in short, is to be used as an open-ended discussion guide in which teachers, through conversation, bring their knowledge and experience to bear on the fundamental issues raised in this book. Through these conversations, teachers may, in a true sense, talk and think their way to their own "book" on teaching.

This book is an invitation to think and talk about ways for teachers and students to create a school that honors one's mind — a place that asks the "why" questions, that engages teachers in critical conversation, and that seeks out and argues the merits of various teaching practices.

2. *What Every Great Teacher Knows* was written — we shall be blunt — to provide an antidote to the intellectual vacuity of most methods books on teaching and the offensive recipes for teaching offered in almost all inservice programs (Campbell 1989, pp. 114-117). We also want to avoid the academic posturing of books that claim to make teaching a "science" based on the nonscientific findings of research on teaching.[1]

Until the education of teachers moves toward its intellectual and artistic base, teaching will be lost in the sinister alleys of technique isolated from thought. Thought and practice — doing teaching — are not fierce competitors for your attention; each needs the other, each enriches the other. So long as teachers themselves pine for the easy fix of technique cut off from ideas, there will be no end of entertaining charlatans willing to provide a fix — for a high fee. Our obsession with techniques raises doubts when we rightfully claim that teaching is a profession.

The import of these two purposes is to make *What Every Great Teacher Knows* a different kind of book; it is not a methods book although it deals with teaching; it is not an academic book *about* teaching, or the present state of teaching in America, because we want you to use the ideas and stories in *What Every Great Teacher Knows* to explore your own teaching. This journey may lead to other books and experiences that will further deepen your appreciation of the teacher's art. There are many technocrats in business and the information technologies who can't wait to displace your humanness with one of their computers and an interactive video.

Teachers now and in the future will have to be able to give *reasoned* explanations why certain ways of teaching are better than other ways.

To speak of informed conversation as an important way to improve the quality of schools and teacher education sounds terribly old-fashioned in this day of high-tech buzz words and slick commercial programs. Talk — sustained, informed talk about learning and teaching — is a rare visitor to faculty meetings or to staff development programs. This assertion is validated both by many teachers' experience as well as by the research of such investigators as John Goodlad (1984). In *A Place Called School*, Goodlad reports that he and his colleagues rarely found school faculties giving *sustained* attention to *significant* school-wide problems of learning and teaching, despite his finding that overconcern with facts and routine textbook learning deadened the intellectual quality of what was learned and taught. Other educators speak to this unfortunate condition and provide some evidence of the benefits of serious dialogue (see Barth 1990; Brown 1991; Gibboney 1994; Little 1986; Webb et al. 1996).

A TEACHER SAYS "ENOUGH IS ENOUGH"

Patrick Welsh is a high school English teacher in Alexandria, Virginia, who has spoken out against the corruption of teaching and the harassment of teachers when school boards and administrators go all out for the easy fixes promised by slickly packaged techniques. Welsh (1986) cites incident after incident in his book, *Tales Out of School*, where teachers have been forced to ignore their own intelligence and instincts for a "new" way of teaching by administrators (who, themselves, too often avoid the messiness of thinking deeply about teaching by adopting a "program" they picked up in a two-day smoothly presented workshop 500 miles from their schools).

Welsh tells how a teacher evaluation plan adopted by the Alexandria schools in 1984 demoralized good teachers. Teachers, for example, had to have a "sponge activity"[2] (giving kids a short assignment to keep them from talking with each other when they entered a classroom) and a "closure activity" that neatly summed up a 50-minute lesson. Welsh protested. "Why," he asked, "should I be forced to go through a set of prescribed mechanistic procedures" merely to show the public that the school system was trying to improve teaching? The attitude of the principal, when confronted with this and other teachers' objections, seemed to be "I've got the latest secret about teaching — you don't" (Welsh 1986, pp. 168-169).

Welsh distrusted the assumption that "desirable teaching procedures ... could be boiled down to a single Xeroxed page [by which to evaluate a teacher]" (p. 170).

Another teacher wrote in protest that "the evaluation process is like writing a review of a play [after seeing] one or two acts. There is no awareness of [the teacher's] long-term goals...." (Welsh, p. 170).

The technique package Welsh is criticizing swept the country in the 1980s (and continues to have an influence) as "Elements of Effective Instruction" or simply as Madeline Hunter's model. The tragedy is that relatively few teachers and principals had any *idea* that this plan was an educational fraud on students and teachers if the cultivation of the mind is the primary aim of education, as John Dewey (and common sense) states.

Teachers eager for mechanistic techniques to use on their students will surely suffer when their "superiors" use mechanistic techniques on them. Both teachers and administrators who cry only for the "practical" (technique) in easy-to-swallow two-day inservice packages, are the ones who avoid serious informed discussion of *fundamental* issues in learning, teaching, and teacher evaluation. "Too boring," they say. "Let's get practical!" is the cry. We've heard it often in dialogues with teachers and their principal. This cry is the death blow to informed conversation. It makes a joke of teaching as an intellectual activity.

DEWEY'S THEORY

The eighteen principles in this book are fundamental ideas about teaching. They are rooted in John Dewey's theory of education and our own humbling experience over decades in which we used Dewey's theory as a compass in our public school and university teaching, in formal teacher education programs, and, richest of all, when we "left" the low oxygen altitudes of the university to work as peers with hundreds of teachers and their principals on *their* turf to help them make their schools more intellectually stimulating places.

Why Dewey's theory and not someone else's? "Surely there are other theories comparable to his" is a common response to our belief that Dewey's *educational* theory is superior to all others. Consider the theories we are rejecting. Plato is the first to go (philosopher-kings do not fit well with the U.S. Constitution). Theories based on any sectarian religion fail to meet our democratic criterion. Out go the mechanistic conditioning learning theories of E. L. Thorndike and B. F. Skinner and a legion of followers. Robert Hutchins and the Great Books, solid as they are, do not meet our criterion of comprehensiveness. What about Piaget, or Abraham Maslow and the humanistic psychologists, or Karl Marx or Michel Foucault? Why not Howard Gardner and multiple intelligences or Leslie Hart's theory based on brain research or — the favorite of many educational psychologists and educational researchers — collections of empirical research studies such as those on "effective teaching" that Barak Rosenshine and Madeline Hunter accept? Sorry, but none of these even come close to being an acceptable theory of *education* in a democratic society.

We accept Dewey's theory because it is the only one that meets the following three major criteria of usefulness.

1. A useful theory of education must be comprehensive rather than partial (one that deals with only *some* of the elements that should be treated in a comprehensive theory). Piaget, for example, deals with the intellectual development of mathematical concepts among others, but he is silent about the nature of the society in which the learning child lives. Thus, his theory is limited; nor does he think of himself primarily as an educator (Elkind 1970, p. 81). (Since "comprehensiveness" is a critically important criterion, we illustrate more completely in the next section what comprehensiveness means in Dewey's theory when he puts the theoretical light on thinking.)

2. A useful theory must commit its adherents to the intellectual growth of teachers *and* students; further, the theory must reasonably suggest how and why this growth ought to occur and what it looks like in the real world of day-to-day living.

3. A useful theory of education must be consistent with democratic values and show how education in a democratic society may help students and teachers to become both critics and intelligent shapers of their society, the outcome of which is surely unknowable and the success of which is ever in doubt. One is always running with uncertainty in a democratic state (which is one practical reason why teachers and principals need to encourage student initiative and responsibility and not be "spooked" into rigidity by ambiguity and the shades of gray that exist in any subject matter honestly pursued. Year after year of tight and tidy lesson plans, such as those based on the weak research on effective teaching, stunt the mind and sterilize the democratic spirit).

In short, if the complexities of education are thought of as a novel, Dewey's novel has a complex cast of believable characters, a good plot, and, best of all, there are no essential chapters missing. Dewey does not retreat before the *complexity* of the problems he chooses to address, as do weaker theorists and most empirical researchers in learning, teaching, or school reform policy. The empirical research approach to "theory" has given us hurtful "theories" such as Direct Teaching, Madeline Hunter, and the "thinking skills" embarrassment. All of these prescriptions de-skill teaching and routinize learning. Dewey wisely avoids the empirical research trap in his theorizing.

A Short Illustration of Dewey's "Comprehensiveness" in Thinking

Dewey's theory directs the compass of ideas in *What Every Great Teacher Knows* because Dewey's is the only comprehensive theory of education we have that is hospitable to two important values — the cultivation of teachers' and students' intelligence *and* democratic values. These two values are linked with each other; they are not separate fragments as in lesser, partial theories. Without the ability to consider social problems such as poverty, for example, or the decline of well-paying jobs for our youth in whatever "track" their high school might have put them, the quality of democratic life is reduced or threatened. To solve a significant problem that is important to society and which helps the problem solver to grow is one facet of thinking in Deweyan terms.

A good comprehensive theory makes larger and clearer *patterns* from the scattered pieces of experience; bad theories take legitimate pieces of education such as cooperation, discipline, motivation, multiculturalism, or even thinking and break them into even smaller pieces called skills. Thus, we have kits that purport to teach the skills of reading; to teach the skills of cooperative learning (which is primarily a means and not a major educational end in itself); to teach the skills of classroom management; to teach the skills of teaching and so on, world without end. In a comprehensive theory such as Dewey's, skills are there, of course, information and facts are there (one cannot think without content, i.e., something to think *with*), *but ideas are there too.*

Dewey's "theory of thinking," which is a major element in his larger theory, is indeed comprehensive. Dewey first places thinking in a social context: democratic society. Thinking, then, is an individual act that relates to and affects others. Most psychological theories of thinking, in contrast, view thinking as an individual act rather than an act that is both an individual and a social phenomenon. It is easy to see why Dewey opposed IQ testing in the 1920s in *The New Republic,* when many of his peers were mesmerized by this latest "scientific wonder" from psychology. Intelligence testing, Dewey feared, would limit individual growth and serve undemocratic elite interests. History has confirmed his judgment.

Dewey makes other connections with what otherwise would be unrelated pieces in weak theories:

- Thinking is in one's ordinary life experience and requires action, a trying out of possible solutions to a problem.

- The intellectual value of an experience or learning is in the cumulative increase in wider relationships and meaning one perceives.

- In education words often obscure ideas because there is no action by the learner — a trying out — that might make the consequences of an idea known.

- Thinking begins with an uncertain, problematic situation, something incomplete and unfulfilled.

- Thinking implies some emotional concern with an issue or a problem.

- Acquiring knowledge and skills is always secondary to the act of inquiring, i.e., problem solving.

- All thinking results in knowledge, but the ultimate value of knowledge is that it aids thinking because the world is an unsettled place.

Dewey states that in education the primary goal of teaching is thinking: "… all [that] the school can or need do for pupils, so far as their *minds* are concerned … is to develop the ability to think" (Dewey 1916, p. 152, emphasis in original). Dewey put thinking first in 1916, but this profundity seems to have passed over us in the ensuing eight decades.

The quality of the problem generated is the most important thing one can ask of an educational experience, Dewey states. No amount of improved teacher technique will compensate for a poor classroom environment in which there is little stuff (Dewey's word) to stimulate thought; stuff like workbenches and wood, laboratory equipment, things and social situations that cause one to think in ways that are more like ordinary life outside school. The material of thinking is not thoughts, "but actions, facts, events, and the relations of things" (p. 156). Facts, data, and knowledge lead to conjectured meanings, tentative explanations, possible relationships of piece A to piece F and piece X — in short, ideas, according to Dewey.

Another example of comprehensiveness is a favorite of both students and teachers in the field: "No thought, no idea, can possibly be conveyed as an idea from one person to another. When it is told, it is, to the one to whom it is told, [just] another given fact, not an idea" (p. 159). Try to find something that profound in your thinking skills kit! This quotation itself is well worth discussion in several class sessions because it says that *ideas* cannot be given from teacher to student merely through teacher talk.

One last quotation from *Democracy and Education*, also a favorite: Dewey first says that facts and information alone merely locate the problem and help to clarify it. Data may stimulate possible solutions. Data — bits of information — represent what is settled and known about the problem. Dewey then makes a further point that is of fundamental importance to our fact-bound, information-overloaded schools: Inferences drawn from data suggest possible results or things to do, not facts that are already known. "Inference is always an invasion of the unknown, a leap from the known" (p. 158). Is it not understandable why teachers and principals in our democratic and commercially restricted culture might tread lightly on the cultivation of thought? How many teachers (or lawyers or craftsmen or professors) dare too often to think and mount "an invasion of the unknown"? To think may endanger one's career.

Go back over the example. How many otherwise loose educational "colors" such as data, action, and inference, to cite only three, does Dewey tie together to make a larger, more colorful quilt of thinking? This is what comprehensiveness means. Good theories try for an elegant simplicity. Physicists dream of one final theory that will explain the physical universe. Good theories go for unified wholes, not tortuously patched together, incoherent pieces of wholes.

How to Use This Guide

In the preceding section we argued briefly that the primary goal of Dewey's theory is to encourage thought among teachers, principals, and students. If teachers or principals are unthinking and too routinized in their work, it is unlikely that the students they teach will make conjectures or critically review data in a subject field, and so forth. Thinking adults within a school environment give the cultivation of intelligence a big assist, although this "teaching resource" is shamefully neglected in most preservice and in virtually all inservice education. Thinking teachers are worth more than the most expensive computers in a school (and teachers are not sent to the scrap heap as quickly).

Since thinking permeates Dewey's theory, we intend each of the 18 principles to throw some light on one or more aspects of thought. So our first suggestion on how to use this guide is that *all* of the principles speak to some aspect of thinking as worked out in Dewey's theory. If you are interested in improving the quality of your teaching with respect to thinking, you might scan the informal wording of each principle listed in the Table of Contents. Your eye might fall on Principle 2, which speaks of encouraging students to ask questions rather than only the teacher asking "pat" questions of students. The second tale under Principle 2 is an interview with Alfie Kohn, who tells of his struggles as a teacher to give students more *real* choices in school as one way of developing student initiative and responsibility. His account tells how he dealt with a "bad" English class and the "solid wall of hostility [he] met in that classroom." Classroom management techniques were not helpful, but a change to a "curriculum worth learning" did help. There is much to think about in this teacher's story.

Principles 13 and 14 state that the total classroom environment educates and that if teachers teach too directly for results — memorization and drill for a test — they short-circuit thought. The tales show how one group of elementary teachers in a school-based dialogue created a better learning environment by reorganizing their curriculum around unifying themes that permitted some correlation of content among several subjects. The second tale tells how Susan Moon, a veteran Foxfire teacher in rural Georgia, has made the transition from traditional teaching to Foxfire's more holistic approach. Ms. Moon captures the spirit of her teaching when she shows how she brings in interesting real-life experiences — such as mentoring projects with elementary students — to create a total classroom environment that encourages student initiative, writing, and thinking.

We have found that sometimes it is one line in a tale, the comments that precede the tale, or an experience or idea recalled by a teacher in a dialogue group, that sparks an insight related to the thrust of the principle itself. One should read the comments and stories in this book in a relaxed, creative attitude. You will not always find a neat, one-to-one correspondence between the content of the tales, the comments, and the principle; but if you approach them imaginatively and broadly as you read and discuss them, you will always find something in the story or in the principle that should spark a fruitful conversation. In this way teachers using this guide to more thoughtful teaching can "write" their own version as they read and discuss the principles in their education courses or in school-based inservice sessions.

The principles truly contain profound, although out-of-fashion, ideas for academia and for schools. As Dewey says, we cannot "give you" a complex idea by words alone; to you it is only one more burdensome, isolated fact — it becomes merely another entry in your education encyclopedia. More academic exposition here will only obscure the ideas and keep you from your initial engagement with them. *So you (as will your own students) sneak up on these elusive tigers in the conceptual jungle the only way you can: you read, you discuss, you debate various meanings and applications, you try some out until — slowly — over time these ideas slip into your mind and grow as your own* experience *becomes richer and as you construct ever better conceptual nets to snare the always elusive tiger.*

A Little More Help to Get Started

Since *What Every Great Teacher Knows* is a book to stimulate thought and discussion among preservice and inservice teachers — an intellectual element which John Goodlad has found is pushed aside for ever more technique — it need not be read "front to back" as other books usually are. The lean format and content of this book are intentional. We want to make it more likely that a *theory-centered* book might take its complementary place among other more traditional methods texts. Teaching and public education desperately need to mend their intellectual fences — and more professors of education need to be in the front ranks of this reform, along with teachers themselves and those principals and superintendents who can manage, yes, but who are educators enough to know that the end of management is not managemen itself. (See Raymond Callahan's 1962 *Education and the Cult of Efficiency* for a classic exposition of how American schools were modeled on factories to increase schools' efficiency and productivity.)

To make it easier for you to get into this book and to see what light *What Every Great Teacher Knows* may cast on a concern you have, or to get another slant on a topic of interest such as school structure or small group work, we offer below an illustrative index to some of the important topics treated. Pick a topic, jump in, read a few of the principles and tales that relate to it and see what you think. Remember that this book is a *guide* to thinking about better teaching through seminal *ideas* invigorated through discussion with your peers and tested for usefulness by you in your own classroom. This is not another book *about* education; this is a book that *does* education.

"Fishing around" in the topic-principle index is the best way to begin using *What Every Great Teacher Knows*. "Fishing around" in the index, choosing the principles and tales you may want to scan, requires an action on your part — which is what Deweyan theory holds is true for learning at any level or any age. The learner (with some assistance from a teacher or, in this case, a book) must *himself* forge some *imaginative link* with the lesson or the book's contents; that is, he approaches the content with a question in mind; e.g., "Yeah. I hear a lot about 'motivation.' We had a workshop on it last year. What do these guys have to say about it? Will it help me?" A preservice teacher might muse as she picks up this book, "We heard in another course that teachers talk too much — about 70% of the time. But what's the corrective? Maybe if we encouraged more student responsibility and initiative over the six years of elementary school, there would be less need for teachers to talk too much. I think I'll take a look at that topic."

None of this is dazzling, but it *is* fundamental. Making American schools as good as they can be requires initiative from more teachers and principals. This book is lean in words and simple in format to encourage you to be more active — to exercise initiative — because this is a quality good teachers have. We want you to engage this book actively in the same way that whole language teaching theory encourages your students to be active rather than passive readers.

GETTING STARTED:
AN ILLUSTRATIVE INDEX OF TOPICS AND
RELATED PRINCIPLES AND STORIES

Topic	Principles
Testing; Assessing Learning	1. The Cultivation of Thinking 3. Never Underestimate What is Involved in Knowing Something Well 6. Objectives Suggest the Learning Environment 7. The What and How of Learning 13. Good Methods Shape the Whole School Environment 14. Real Learning Cannot Be Hurried
Learning	1. The Cultivation of Thinking 5. The Connection Between Thinking and Doing 6. Objectives Suggest the Learning Environment 7. The What and How of Learning 10. Essential Content is Knowledge of General Social Significance 11. Your Community is an Essential Content Source 13. Good Methods Shape the Whole School Environment
Motivation	1. The Cultivation of Thinking 5. The Connection Between Thinking and Doing 8. Objectives Must be Tied to Larger Aims 9. Teaching Objectives Need to Make Sense to the Learner 18. Teachers Guide Students Towards Larger Perspectives
School Structure	4. The Importance of Foresight, Purpose, and Reflection 10. Essential Content is Knowledge of General Social Significance 11. Your Community is an Essential Content Source 12. The Purpose of Education is Not Fact-Gathering but Inquiry and Meaning-Making
Small Group Work	6. Objectives Suggest the Learning Environment 7. The What and How of Learning 9. Teaching Objectives Need to Make Sense to the Learner 13. Good Methods Shape the Whole School Environment 14. Real Learning Cannot Be Hurried 17. The Contribution of the Individual to the Group — and the Group to the Individual

Topic	Principles
Relating Content to Students' Lives	2. The Value of Questions 3. Never Underestimate What Is Involved in Knowing Something Well 4. The Importance of Foresight, Purpose, and Reflection 5. The Connection Between Thinking and Doing 15. Real Learning Starts With Ordinary Problems
Democratic Values	2. The Value of Questions 8. Objectives Must be Tied to Larger Aims 10. Essential Content is Knowledge of General Social Significance 11. Your Community is an Essential Content Source 13. Good Methods Shape the Whole School Environment 14. Real Learning Cannot be Hurried
Organizing the Curriculum	7. The What and How of Learning 8. Objectives Must be Tied to Larger Aims 9. Teaching Objectives Need to Make Sense to the Learner 10. Essential Content is Knowledge of General Social Significance 11. Your Community is an Essential Content Source 13. Good Methods Shape the Whole School Environment 14. Real Learning Cannot Be Hurried
Student Responsibility and Initiative	2. The Value of Questions 3. Never Underestimate What is Involved in Knowing Something Well 6. Objectives Suggest the Learning Environment 10. Essential Content is Knowledge of General Social Significance 11. Your Community is an Essential Content Source 16. Abstract Ideas Need to be Applied in Practical Contexts
Teacher/Student Planning	2. The Value of Questions 3. Never Underestimate What Is Involved in Knowing Something Well 13. Good Methods Shape the Whole School Environment 14. Real Learning Cannot Be Hurried 15. Real Learning Starts With Ordinary Problems

FOUR ARBITRARY CATEGORIES OF TEACHING

For convenience and simplicity, we have organized the principles, comments, and tales into four functional categories. In real teaching and in Deweyan theory, of course, all of the four categories interact and simultaneously influence each other as a learning experience unfolds. With this caution in mind, the four categories may lend a legitimate simplicity to the complex social interaction we call teaching. Thinking and Experience contains five principles; Teaching Objectives, four; Subject Matter, three; and Teaching Methods, six.

A PRACTICAL APPLICATION: PRINCIPLE 7

Principle 7 states, *"The [teaching] objectives value both what is to be learned and how it is to be learned. [Objectives reflect the understanding that] the quality of learning is critically dependent on how the objective is achieved."*

The unwarranted separation of the "what" and "how" in learning and teaching is a feature of many reforms advanced by legislatures, reform commissions, and university researchers to the perceived problem that students are not achieving well in school.[3] A clear example of the separation of the "what" from the "how" is illustrated by the "thinking skills" movement, an expert-driven effort that separates thinking from content. For example, two widely-known "thinking skills" programs, CoRT and Instrumental Enrichment, define thinking as skills, i.e., what one does when one thinks. The presumed skills of thinking (CoRT defines 60) are taught as separate subjects in both programs; that is, the skills taught become a new subject with unique content that is *added* to the curriculum (Thrush 1987, pp. 133-170).

The companion phenomenon of "critical thinking" may suffer from the same limitation: Many supporters of critical thinking treat its subject matter as an add-on to the regular curriculum (see, for example, Paul 1992), similar to CoRT and Instrumental Enrichment. Critical thinking is considered to be new knowledge, requiring the mastery of logical rules as well as numerous "strategies." Later, its proponents say, critical thinking will be brought to bear on other school subjects (as well as on life's problems). One more "extra" for busy teachers to worry about.

The aim of programs such as these is worthy; however, a problem arises when thinking — even critical thinking — is defined in terms of *arbitrary "skills" separated from opportunities to think that arise in learning the content in the school's regular curriculum.* This separation violates

Principle 7 that hinges on the subtle *quality* relationship between *how* we learn something and the *thing* learned — the learning outcome. Principle 7 suggests that educators use care both in selecting *what* is to be learned and deciding *how* it is to be taught. The isolation of thinking from the content of the curriculum is undesirable.[4]

Further, CoRT and Instrumental Enrichment do not agree, even broadly, on what the skills of thinking are.[5] Finally, they are taught in a drill-like fashion that markedly reduces flexibility for the teacher and the student. We believe that the application of Principle 7 to the teaching of thinking leads to the conclusion that a faulty definition of "what" is to be taught — skills — isolates thinking from the curriculum, which leads to the mechanical teaching of fragmented bits of (supposedly) "skilled" knowledge. These programs permit little flexibility in the ways the skills are to be learned (the "how" of learning). The two programs, in sum, define thinking as a skill that creates a falsely efficient learning process.

The ideas expressed in Principle 7 (and in all the other principles) are useful. They can serve our practical interest by helping us avoid the pitfalls of the thinking skills and critical thinking fads.

WHY DO TEACHERS TALK TOO MUCH?

A final illustration follows to show how teachers' comments that arise in discussion are relevant to the principles we have proposed. This example comes from a verbatim excerpt from a dialogue session in the Lower Merion School District, Lower Merion, Pennsylvania. We eavesdropped here on 20 high school teachers and their principal and vice principal who are using dialogue as a fundamental reform process (Bolton 1994, pp. 390-415; Gibboney 1994, pp. 205-207). The question that had arisen from a discussion of *Horace's Compromise* is, why do teachers talk about 70% of the time when they are "teaching"? (Lower Merion is one of the wealthiest school districts in Pennsylvania. We note this fact to suggest that money alone does not wash away the need to confront basic issues arising in learning and teaching in any school that hopes to become a more thoughtful place.)

Teacher: The readings say that changing the structure of a school means more staff involvement. Now one thing that hit me in the readings is that teachers need more involvement, interaction with their students. So conceptually we are talking about the same idea for kids that we are talking about for teachers. The same idea works both ways, it seems to me.

Teacher: But when we are dealing with teachers and administrators we are dealing with adults about professional things. Dealing with kids is different.

Teacher: I disagree. We stand up front and lecture. We do "top down." But I know why. It's what we are supposed to do — it's what teaching is to the students. They want me to learn it for them.

[The discussion continued with neither teachers nor administrators willing to make an educated guess on the amount of teacher talk in the school.]

Moderator: Let's take humanities — your fields. How much do teachers talk in your subjects?

Teacher: Well, it depends again. In honors sections, there is more discussion. The regular sections need more direction because of the materials and the students.

Moderator: But those are choices teachers make. There are other choices. Don't you have a gut feeling on teacher talk? Let's walk around 10 minutes on each floor and I'd bet we would know.

Teacher: Okay. There are times when we all talk too much. But I find that to get students to talk takes more time, it's more work with all the other things. When I have more student talk, I run short on time. It is much easier to just tell the kids what's what. Days I talk too much, I feel bad about it.

Moderator: There are lots of influences on teacher talk.

Teacher: That's what everybody ignores in these books and articles. The articles imply that teachers do it on purpose because they don't know better.

Teacher: Isn't it because we want to be in control? There's lots of stuff wrapped up in this one....

This excerpt shows how we let ourselves *unthinkingly* be pushed by time, or by our implicit "theories" about what and how "nonhonors students" can best learn, among other influences. This interior "push" from our unexamined theories most often results in too much teacher talk and a dash for the content-to-be-covered-by-June goal line. Nothing drains the intellectual content from a subject worth learning more than rapid, drill-like coverage. If you want to do only one thing to make your elementary or secondary school more intellectual and democratic (more time for students to talk and explore ideas, for example), SLOW DOWN. You will find, too, that slowing down generates student interest and reduces behavior problems. Slowing down increases your job satisfaction because educationally unproductive pressures to "cover and test" are rechanneled into a more coherent focus on student learning (rather than on teacher teaching). Democracy is served when teachers cultivate responsible independence in students. Excessive teacher talk is one way teachers exert control even when such a high level of control is unnecessary. The Lower Merion teachers were discovering this condition for themselves as they talked.

This dialogue excerpt shows how one tale may suggest many topics worth exploring: the negative power of unexamined "theories"; how reading a serious book informed the teachers' professional intelligence (and serious reading is nonexistent in inservice programs and one has good reason to doubt its presence in many education courses); how community norms influence how teachers teach; changing school structure; the initial reluctance of the teachers and administrators to admit the extent of excessive teacher talk; and the invidious distinction in methods between smart students (they get the more Deweyan method) and the less bright students (they get the good old Thorndike-Skinner-workbook-memorize-and-drill routine — just the ticket for boring them and turning them off to reading and discussion and other intellectual pursuits).

The challenge to reading *What Every Great Teacher Knows* and its practical payoff lies in your (imaginative) ability to make connections such as these with its content — connections that might not be obvious at first glance. And "making connections" is one aspect of thinking that Dewey develops in his theory.

What Every Great Teacher Knows speaks to ideas such as these. They may sound a little strange at first because we are more accustomed to buying ready-made *programs* to solve the practical problems of teaching than we are to weighing *ideas* about teaching. In spite of the uncertainty you may first experience in thinking about these principles, you will be able to construct a thoughtful perspective on teaching. *What Every Great*

Teacher Knows does not oversimplify the complexities of learning and teaching as does much of the research on teacher or school effectiveness. "Rules" based on this research lead to stiff and mechanical actions that will not meet the intellectual and democratic aims that a sound theory of education must endorse.

We hope you will read, discuss, and apply the principles in *What Every Great Teacher Knows* to important problems of learning and teaching in your classroom and school. The book should be used as a "starter kit" to provoke thoughtful talk among teachers and among preservice teachers and professors about learning and about teaching. The talk should be serious and unhurried. Do not rush through the principles in a session or two in a too-quick search for "solutions." Give the ideas time to grow — in your mind and in the minds of colleagues. Remember, learning — your own or your students' — cannot be rushed without a big drop in quality.

Schools are lonely places for too many of us. This need not be so. When teachers and principals come together to engage their minds about the problems we know exist in our schools, our decades-long experience in schools says that not only do they face the intellectual elements in learning, but improvement in teacher and administrator morale results. Teachers and administrators feel less isolated from each other once the conversation is underway, according to our research data (Gibboney 1994, chapters 5 and 6). The consequent enthusiasm, hard won, is beautiful to see but impossible to convey to anyone who has not felt it first-hand. Perhaps this finding confirms part of our conviction that any intellectual effort is accompanied by emotional effects. We hope you'll try serious conversation and see if it works for you.

Part Two

**Eighteen Teaching Principles
With Illustrative Stories**

Thinking and Experience

Dewey (1944/1916) may have said it best: "Thinking is the intentional endeavor to discover specific connections between something which we do and the consequences which result, so that the two become continuous" (p. 145). In other words, thinking is what connects "cause and effect, activity and consequences." Its purpose is control — to increase the degree of an individual's mastery over his or her own destiny. Thinking multiplies our alternatives. Thinking expands insight; expanded insight makes foresight — the agent of control — "more accurate and comprehensive" (p. 145). Thinking and ordinary experience are inextricably connected.

PRINCIPLE 1

EVERY GREAT TEACHER
MAKES THE CULTIVATION OF THINKING
IN A DECENT AND HUMANE ENVIRONMENT
THE PRIMARY GOAL OF TEACHING.

All of the principles in *What Every Great Teacher Knows* speak to elements related to thinking (and to the feelings that always go along with thinking). Because all of the ideas we discuss bear on the intellectual quality of what the teacher does, as well as the quality of the students' thinking and feeling, we will not try to wrap up "thinking" in several easy-to-read pages. Thought is too subtle to treat as a single variable removed from other things that go on in the classroom.

To expand on a topic discussed earlier, when we say "thinking skills," typically lurking in the back of our mind is the idea of discrete, identifiable, and universal actions; behavioral performances at which one is adroit. The lingering learning from our psychology courses reminds us that skill means a smooth and integrated performance of a learned motor activity.[6] The assumption is that such skills exist more or less independently of whether our thinking is about writing a composition, choosing a mate, or understanding a theory in physics or linguistics.

The belief that thinking can be reduced to skills promotes a pedagogy that yields mechanical performances, linear sequences of actions that are assumed to add up to "reading," "critical analysis," or "thinking." But thinking, when we consider it in light of our own experience, is more like creative exploration than something that follows a step-wise sequence.

Perhaps skill is to thinking as the ability to use a dictionary is to an excellent essay. Spelling correctly and hyphenating consistently make the essay better, but alone they contribute little to the ideas, images, and nuances that make the essay worth reading in the first place. If thinking is more than a skill, what might it look like when teachers and students engage in activities that are truly intellectual or thoughtful?

We tell two teachers' tales that bring teaching thinking into the classroom. One teacher's story shows how a change in a science test encouraged thinking; the second story is based on an observer's account of a mathematics teacher, Hal Honig, who creates a "total math environment" in his class that leads students to think — and to enjoy the experience.

The way we test students may encourage or hinder their willingness to think. The following account, reported by Mr. William Rohrer, then Assistant Principal, Penn Manor High School, Millersville, Pennsylvania, makes the point that testing is teaching too.

A Science Test

It is an educational cliché to say that what we test is what we really value. When students ask "What is going to be on the test?" they are really making a statement like this: "What is tested is what is important for me to learn." The content of a test is a mirror that reflects the content that we truly value.

Our ninth-grade Earth Science course was planned so that half of the class time was spent in experiments and demonstrations that made more concrete such ecological forces as acid rain or the influence of the land's physical features on the economic life of the people. These experiments were to be hands-on, synthesizing activities that were made intellectual by using scientific concepts to understand real-life phenomena.

The problem was that the teacher-made tests did not test for this more complex activity. There were no questions, for example, that related the physical properties of acid rain to the social effects of water pollution, to fish kills, or to the stunting of the growth of trees in forest lands. The tests asked for fact recall and ignored the more conceptual and integrative laboratory work that dealt with *science*.

The testing/learning problem was rather easily resolved once it was defined as a problem. The faculty decided to test for two class periods. The first period test was primarily short-answer type questions with some application-of-content questions. The second period test required the student to solve problems. This test was "open book." Students were permitted to bring any material to the test that they thought might be helpful.

While getting the correct solution was important, the students knew that the (quality) of the solution process used was also to be evaluated. This feature of the test reduced the tendency of students to go only for the correct answer, and to see the answer as something isolated from a process of reasoning, by selecting content appropriate to the problem, or using concepts to simplify and make sensible the countless "facts" associated with something as complex as air or water pollution. Half of the student's grade was based on the problem-solving test.

I know that this example is not glamorous or exciting. It cost little in time or money. But it paid a dividend in higher student interest, and in making our testing procedure support the thinking processes that we were spending half of our class time teaching.

How we test is one important element that influences the quality of a classroom or school. Two other elements more directly related to quality are what and how one teaches. Given a limited amount of reform energy and money, if forced to choose, first, we would put our energy into the quality of the educational water entering the upstream end of the pipe, improving the quality of the learning and teaching in a school; second, we would devote our remaining energy to devising ways to assess learning that supported and extended a more intellectual and democratic way of teaching. The following account by a mathematics teacher reflects a mix of thoughtful teaching and, possibly, more conventional testing. After you have read the account, you might ask yourself, and discuss with others, whether Hal Honig is a good "progressive" teacher, a good "traditional" teacher, or some mix of both. (Or maybe even a not-so-good teacher, if you wish.) This account was written by Ms. Johanna Rebarchak, Great Valley High School, Pennsylvania, a colleague of Mr. Honig, who observed the class over several months as a hands-on project for a supervision course.

An Uncommon Classroom

Sunrise at Great Valley High School, Great Valley, Pennsylvania, is an experience. As one looks across the fields from the front door, one feels as if there are no boundaries to the world; everything is open. The trees, hills, and sky are not marred by man-made distractions. It is a picture of beauty and freedom. Sometimes when I arrive in the early morning, I take a moment to stop, turn around, breathe deeply, and capture nature at her best. I feel unlimited possibilities for the day ahead. This sense of beauty, joy, freedom, and growth are feelings that children should have when they enter a school building; these should not be benefits that come only from the outdoors.

As visitors enter, they are greeted with a surprise. The beauty of nature has not been closed off to those within. Inside the front door and ahead is the Senior Court where the sun cascades through glass walls that enclose an outdoor courtyard complete with trees, plants, flowers, and benches. Great Valley High School was built in the 1960s and true to the spirit of the time, combines a mixture of glass and open spaces uncommon to the 1990s-style building. Winding through the maze-like hallways, visitors sense the influence students have at GVHS as evidenced by the displays of their work throughout the building. But we have a destination; let's continue on to Room 104. From the outside it looks like any other classroom, but the similarity ends as one crosses the threshold.

The horizon of the outdoors is captured within the four walls of the classroom. Room 104 holds many possibilities for growth and intellectual stretching; but it is not the physical layout of the room that interests me, but the individual there who guides his students in learning. Hal Honig, an exceptional math teacher by many people's standards, focuses the minds in Room 104 not on "right answers," but on experiencing the complexity and challenge of math.

The room itself is a math teacher's room. The order of the classroom makes me very comfortable. I could learn here. On the solid inside wall above the blackboard there are student-made posters. Opposite is a glass wall with a blackboard running through the middle; in the front of the room is an overhead projector with a screen that always seems to be pulled down. There is Hal's desk, a bookcase with math books, and the students' desks. They are usually facing front for the beginning of the lesson but do not stay that way for long.

The crispness of the winter day hints at a fresh beginning. It is the first class after the midterm exam and the students filter into the room in small groups. "How did you graph number 15?" "Were you able to do the last problem?" "I had a hard time with the graph for that last problem." The bell sounds. The conversation continues as before only with Hal Honig directing its path. "Any questions?" Hal asks. This will become a familiar phrase over the next several weeks. The students respond immediately. It seems that the students are not quite ready to put the past semester in for its winter's nap. Some unfinished business must be settled before they begin the second semester. There is a great deal of interest in reviewing some of the midterm problems. Since GVHS does not return exams to students, they rely on their memories for the problems. In this task they are as crisp as the day. They focus on the content of the exam rather than on their grades.

Hal uses the overhead projector to illustrate, requesting that student talk guide the process. There is a quiet bantering back and forth of ideas between Hal and the students and among the students. Thoughts swirl like the dry, brown leaves outside, blown by the wind. Brad moves quietly to the blackboard to work out a problem: "... $y = x2$ and $y = 4x2$ — here the integral is between 4 and 0. The graph is a parabola...." Hal fields questions about the exam until everyone is satisfied. "Most of you did very well on the exam. Remember our long-term goal is the AP test. We have sixteen sections to cover before the end of the year. We have three months to get it done, so we won't have to fly. Everyone will do okay; don't worry."

The winds of change are sweeping across Room 104; the old is laid to rest, and it is time for the new. The class moves quickly from the past to the present. "Our goal is to identify the Mean Value Theorem for Integrals." Hal spends the next several minutes demonstrating how to derive the formula; the students take notes, commenting casually to one another as the lesson proceeds. "Brad, are you getting this?" Brad may be getting it, but it's Greek to me. Hal assigns a problem, "Do the problem; when you have the answer, raise your hand." Hal quietly canvasses the room, checking individuals for understanding. The students welcome Hal's intrusion into their space. Mark raises his hand then moves quickly to the board. Chantel changes her seat to have a better vantage point from which to see. "The problem is to graph $y = 2x^2 - 2$. The figure is a parabola with the limits of integration of 1/2 and 0," Mark explains. "How many see that?" inquires Hal. As Mark solves the problem, another student who has the answer to Part B puts this section on the blackboard and waits to demonstrate his procedure. Time passes quickly. A homework assignment is given. Hal details what they will be working on the next day, and the bell sounds the end of this class.

A curious occurrence led me to select Mr. Honig as the teacher I would like to observe for my supervision project. As

Resource Room teacher, I have heard just about every negative comment that can be imagined about teachers. Typically, when students are frustrated, unsuccessful, and uninterested, they shift the blame for their failure to the teacher. However, this is not the case with Mr. Honig's students. For example, I have several senior students who are taking Algebra II and experiencing great difficulty. It is necessary for them to pass the course to graduate. This places an inordinate amount of stress on them. Each student displays the effects of stress in a unique way, but one thing is true about all of them — they never blame Mr. Honig for their lack of success. "Mr. Honig cares that I learn, but I can't seem to understand." "He explains it and I ask questions, but I just can't get it." "I just can't see it." Their perception of the problem is self-related. They don't report, "He can't teach," or "He won't let me ask questions," or "He moves too fast." Hearing Mr. Honig's students' comments over several weeks raised this question: What is happening in his classroom that is not happening in other rooms?

On A Clear Day (You Can See Forever)

Calculus is a lot like a winter day — brisk, clear, and predictable. You know the answers by graphing the lines, angles, and curves, using the formulas to solve the problems. Today, there are twenty students in the class — an even mixture of boys and girls. Outside, the chill of winter's breath is in the air; inside, the satisfaction of problems being solved warms the air. Math class, while it does not exude the excitement of a football game, possesses a good feeling of quiet persistence until the goal is reached; this quality generates its own excitement. Entering through the door, Kevin says, "Got that problem!" with a sense of achievement. Several other students gather around him and an animated conversation ensues. The starting bell rings. "How many were successful with those two problems last night?" Hal queries. A show of hands indicates success. "Who has the answer to the first one, $y = x^2$, $y = 4x^2$?" Mark responds in the affirmative and moves to put it on the board. "And the second one?" Laurel goes to the board. Solution procedures are demonstrated by the volunteers with both students and Hal focused on the presenters. Next, Hal moves to the overhead and teacher and students discuss alternative strategies for solving the problems. Hal raises a new problem: "Take this rotten thing [the problem] and solve it in terms of x.... Let's do it." The students put their heads together in quiet conversation to arrive at a solution. Hal randomly moves from group to group commenting here and there, "Yeah" or "Good," sometimes just watching and nodding in assent. "How many are sitting there with the right answer?" Hal asks. A number of students nod in the affirmative.

An unintentional loudspeaker announcement disrupts the moment. The students laugh and there are several moments of chatter. Hal checks the time and draws the students quickly back into focus with a new problem on the overhead. "When you have the integral, let me know." Calculus is back on the agenda. "You can work in groups or on your own. Check page 358 in your text for some other problems.... We won't get through all these today. Ask yourself some questions [as you are going along]." The students spend about fifteen minutes working independently. Periodically, questions are raised; there is a shared sense of ownership of these problems; a quiet "uh-huh" (if I may borrow a phrase from Ray Charles) arises when a solution is reached. Hal calls the group back together. "We will spend Monday, and Tuesday on this." Kevin says, "No homework for the weekend, right?" Hal: "Please attempt every problem — the more you do, the more you get out of it [homework]."

The closing bell sounds. The students are looking forward to seeing lines, angles, and curves all right, but not those of the math problems; rather, they see those of the barren trees and the streets outside as they make their way home for a weekend break. Friday is here — one period down and six more to go.

There is a nice comfort level in this classroom. A rapport exists between the teacher and the students and among the students themselves. It shows itself in a number of ways. There is little standing on ceremony here. Students question the teacher and each other frequently, persisting when they do not understand. The method is more important than the answer; this is obvious to me. A sense of cooperation and sharing prevails. There is no copying of answers here. Let me explain. I am a realist. Some students copy answers when they have not done their homework. This does not seem to be the case in Hal's class. Upon entering the classroom (before the bell) students are already talking easily about the problems they did for homework. They are not saying, "Let me see your answers"; they are saying, "How did you do number 3?" Did you try number 5?" "I had a hard time with number 10." When Mr. Honig asks if anyone has figured out how to do a problem and someone responds positively, the person immediately goes up and puts the problem on the board. Every student who puts a problem on the board explains the thought processes he or she has gone through to solve the problem. Students do not seem to be intimidated by talking in front of their peers. I never heard any snide, critical remarks about anyone, whether the problem was done correctly or not.

What do you think? Does Mr. Honig teach "thinking" in a humane environment?

PRINCIPLE 2

EVERY GREAT TEACHER VALUES AND ENCOURAGES STUDENT QUESTIONING BECAUSE QUESTIONS ENCOURAGE STUDENT AND TEACHER THOUGHT.

If teachers do not help students to inquire on their own, at least to some level, they sever learning from life. This is true because we grow toward intellectual maturity through recognizing, and working to satisfy, our perplexities. J. T. Dillon (1988) points out that perplexity is a "precondition of questioning and thus the *prerequisite* for learning" (p. 18, emphasis added). Without some sense of discrepancy between old and new learning, neither students nor teachers will be provoked to question, much less examine, ideas. This is Dewey's point in *Democracy and Education*: "Where there is reflection there is suspense"; that is, thinking occurs precisely "when things are uncertain or doubtful or problematic" (p. 148). And it is not enough that the *teacher* frame questions by the dozen, because those questions may not be the *learner's* questions. Unless the learner herself raises questions, no meaningful learning can occur. Answers are not enough, either: You cannot give an answer to someone who has not asked the question. The idea that school teaching and learning are best conceived as a perplexity-free and learner-inquiry-free effort has resulted in the "trivialization of valuable knowledge, habits of mind, and skills" (Lanier and Sedlak 1989, p. 119).

The following two tales illustrate important facets of Principle 2. The first shows what an eight-year-old student has learned about asking questions in school. The second illustration suggests the importance of greater student initiatives in learning, which includes the opportunity for students to pose questions about what they might learn and why it would be worthwhile to learn it. The interview with Alfie Kohn is about student choice in learning. This interview was conducted by Sara Day Hatton, editor of Foxfire's excellent magazine, *The Active Learner: A Foxfire Journal for Teachers.* This interview was published in the March 1997 issue of *The Active Learner.*

Mrs. Lillian Zarndt, a mother and the owner of a primary school in Springville, Utah, offers the following conversation with her eight-year-old daughter. The story demonstrates how easy it is for hard-working teachers to neglect the cultivation of thinking in their classes.

"Mom, You Don't Get It"

Elizabeth: Mom, do numbers ever end?

Mom: Wow! That's a really neat question. Even people who have studied math all their life wonder about a question like that ... (we go into a long discussion about the pro's and con's of this idea). Did you have math today?

Elizabeth: Um-hm.

Mom: What wonderful questions did you ask in school today?

Elizabeth: I didn't.

Mom: Why not?

Elizabeth: M-o-m (she rolls her eyes in exasperation), you just don't get it. School isn't the place to ask questions.

Teachers "teach" students not to ask questions by indirectly — and unknowingly — discouraging them. This action alone markedly lowers the quality of the classroom environment. But the lowered "thinking quality" of the environment does not stop here. Since twenty students are not asking questions in a class, there are fewer ways for the teacher to get clues firsthand that reveal student interests or their understanding of what is being taught. Even more damaging in this question-free environment is that students have fewer opportunities to explore alternative ways of doing things, or to creatively "play" with an idea or a problem. And, too, the students' use of oral language is reduced when it need not be. The language loss further reduces the intellectual quality of whatever a teacher might teach.

If, on the other hand, one teaches in a Deweyan-progressive way — that is, thoughtfully — giving due regard to the students' interests and needs but not to the exclusion of intellectual growth and teacher guidance, an attitude of questioning often prevails. Alfie Kohn gives some practical advice in the interview that follows on how teachers might make their teaching more thoughtful and thus encourage a higher and more satisfying intellectual exchange in their classrooms.

Offering Challenges, Creating Cognitive Dissonance: An Interview with Alfie Kohn

by Sara Day Hatton
(Editor of *The Active Learner:
A Foxfire Journal for Teachers*)
Introduction by Julia Osteen

Squirming in my seat, I turned the pages of the article very slowly, one by one, until I had read the entire contents. I immediately proceeded to read it again. I experienced feelings which ranged from outrage to embarrassment to disbelief. The article was "Choices for Children: Why and How to Let Students Decide." The experience was my first contact with the beliefs of Alfie Kohn. The problem with the article was that it was all too true. He made me look at situations that occurred in the classroom in a much different light.

Punished by Rewards was my next encounter with his beliefs. Again, he made me think about my interactions with children in a way that was different. Since then I no longer use an individual reward/behavior management system in my classroom. My students and I conference weekly regarding behavior. These conferences are individual and a documentation of the conference goes home to the parent on a form which contains our class agreements. When children ask me "Did I do a good job?" (like little kids will often do), I ask them "What do you think?" I am nowhere near the ideal that Kohn espouses; however, I am closer than before.

In the following interview, he challenges all teachers to examine their beliefs and practices. He provides food for thought and not just oatmeal but steak! It takes a lot of chewing before you can swallow. Enjoy!

Q: At Foxfire, student choice is extremely important in all we do. When did you become aware of the need for student choice, and what are some of the ways you involved your students in your classes?

A: I became aware of most of what students need after I taught, I'm sorry to report. I did several things that in retrospect gave me some source of satisfaction or pride but a lot more that make me wince when I look back on how little I knew about what teachers ought to do. I brought students in, for the most part, in a peripheral way in deciding how they would respond to an essay question or to pick from a range of questions when it was time for assessment, because that was all I knew; it was all that I had experienced from elementary school to graduate school. I missed the point about how important it is for kids to have substantial amounts of discretion in figuring out what they are going to learn and how and why. I came to that belatedly from watching teachers who were much better than I was, reading research and other people's views from Dewey to the present day, and thinking about it a lot. Were I to go back in the classroom today, I would certainly do things differently.

Q: In witnessing other teachers, did you observe obstacles they encountered and can you tell us how they dealt with them?

A: One major impediment to giving students choice is the teacher's own reservations about it. There's no magic solution for someone who isn't sure this is going to work except to be in a community of adults who can talk together at regular intervals about what they are doing and to complain and to search for solutions together and to visit each other's classrooms. I think some of the best teachers are those who are lucky enough to be in the best schools and are able to do that. Another obstacle is that the students themselves are unaccustomed to freedom and react at least at first by engaging in more kinds of behavior, good and bad, than ever before because the controls have finally been loosened. They're able to exercise their autonomy for the first time and that's messy and noisy and aggravating. The teachers I've talked to always suggest patience and also bringing the students in on this very problem. Then if, for example, students make ridiculous choices or sit there paralyzed, unable to do anything except to say "You're the teacher; this is your job," the great teachers are able to react without resentment and too much confusion. They say, "What a great topic for discussion! What's my job? How do you feel when someone tells you what to do all day? Will you say you're too young to make decisions?" Or if students are sitting there impassive during class, that opens all kinds of possibilities, providing the teacher can figure out why this is happening. Is it because they don't feel safe in this classroom? If so, how can we — underline we — change this situation so that nobody is afraid of being left out? If students are sitting there quietly because they have nothing to say at the moment, then forcing them to speak up is worse than doing nothing. If they're merely shy by temperament, that leads you to react in a very different way than if they don't feel their comments are going to be taken seriously.

I think most teachers who have tried to give students choices have realized that the worst of all possible courses is to ask their opinion and then dismiss it. For example, by saying they haven't made a responsible choice, which means they haven't done what the teacher wanted and that therefore their decision doesn't count, they feel used and therefore are unlikely to make that mistake again.

There are educators, William Glasser among them, who talk about the importance of class meetings and inspire teachers to try it out. Often they don't realize just how difficult that transition can be, especially when students are accustomed to being rewarded and punished into compliance and simply told what to do all their lives. You can't go from 0 to 60 overnight, and I always advise teachers to start out easily with a decision or a question that is circumscribed and the results of which they can live with until they are able to fashion with the students a classroom that's more democratic.

I made a few efforts along those lines when I was teaching. I gave them the chance to write in journals back before that was fashionable. I'm not sure if it was the dimension of choice to make the decision about what to write, or what made that such a good decision. It opened up a new world to me of the students' inner lives. I went from looking at the surface of the ocean to becoming Jacques Cousteau, explorer of the deep, where even students who had never come up to talk to me and who would not feel safe talking in front of their peers about the things that gripped their inner lives were opening up to me. If only because it created a kind of relationship under the surface or alongside our public life in the classroom, it was a valuable decision, and the only restraint I put on the journals was that they be something more than a dry chronicle of events. They had to talk about how they thought or felt about what was going on and, of course, I promised them confidentiality, and that stuff was far richer and more meaningful to them than almost anything I was doing in the regular curriculum.

Q: Did you encounter obstacles?

A: With the journals, no, primarily not. But I wish I had done more along those lines so that I could have had to work through obstacles I know good teachers do every day. It took me some years to figure this out but I had the idea when I was teaching high school that a course was something a teacher developed on his or her own, built in the garage and polished like an automobile and took pride in as I did in one course that I taught for many years on existentialism. I honed that reading list, I carefully constructed the balance of activities in the class, and the papers to assign and the reading. Then I took it out of the garage when it was time to teach and brought it out to the students. It took me many years to figure out that as good a course as that was or as exciting a reading list that it had, I didn't understand the first thing about teaching, because it made approximately as much sense to think of a course that way as it would for a single person to say that "I have this great marriage waiting — I can't wait to meet somebody to be my husband or wife and take part in it with me."

It was based on a fallacious view of learning. There is no course until the students and you create it together and I didn't see that when I was teaching. When you get right down to it, either you believe the course is fully formed and delivered to the students or you realize there is nothing but a framework and hunches and first starts and the course itself is created together. I think I see it now but I didn't then. It's not just a matter of how much choice about what books they're going to read; it is a matter of a philosophy of teaching. So a lot of the bumps and barriers and obstacles that great teachers encounter, I, like the great majority of teachers, never had to contend with because I was not teaching authentically to begin with. That's a hard thing for me to admit, and I can only say I wish I had seen it sooner.

Q: Many of our readers are trying to implement learner-centered classrooms such as you describe in your writing. However, they tell us they feel isolated in teaching environments that are not supportive. In your own work, have there been times when you felt this isolation and lack of support and can you give us specific examples?

A: I taught one year at a small independent school in rural Pennsylvania where, even despite all my failings I described, I was the only person even doing rudimentary progressive things; and I had no support whatsoever for that. This was a girl's school and I was the closest thing to a feminist on campus. I think it was the social and political challenge I posed that isolated me more than my pedagogical practice, in part because of how reactionary and cloistered a community it was.

Q: How did you get through that?

A: By keeping my own journal and talking to myself because there was no one to talk to. I wrote letters to my friends and read voraciously but my frustration was poured out into the pages of what turned out to be a book-length manuscript about what I was facing. I draw material from that year that I still remember and that has informed my thinking since then.

I'll give you one example which I have thought about often. I had one class that year where the kids gave me a terrible time. They, as I see it, must have stayed up nights trying to figure out how to make my life a living hell because they couldn't have been that good at it spontaneously. And I'm able to laugh about it now but I was reduced almost to tears sometimes because of the solid wall of hostility I met in that classroom. I thought I was doing things right, you know. I didn't just give them Wordsworth to read, I would give them Joni Mitchell, and I might as well have given them Hegel in the original German. At one point, I said, "Fine, you find me the song lyrics and you can teach them."

But that didn't change the atmosphere in the classroom — it came no closer to creating a situation where we were on a mission of learning together. If you had asked me then what I needed, I would have replied in an instant that I needed a classroom management system, a way to discipline these kids who were obstreperous and noncompliant. What I realize now is I really needed a curriculum worth learning. For the most part, I was using Warriner's, which is essentially "Our Friend, the Adverb" stuff that few members of our species would find intrinsically motivating. And I resorted, to my later shame, to the Grade Book, that combination of bribes and threats to make them learn this material. What I realized much later was that I needed for them to have more choices; I needed a more accurate view of how learning happens and the respects in which students have to construct meaning for themselves instead of swallowing whole the ideas and skills offered to them by a teacher. So that one experience has colored my view of classroom management and the respects in which it is inextricable from and largely a function of the academic learning that is going on in a classroom.

Q: As teachers we really struggle with how we can help students learn to make good choices. Have you struggled with that, and what is your thinking on it?

A: Well, the first step in making a good choice is to have a choice rather than being told what to do most of the time. Kids learn to make good decisions by making decisions, not by following directions. If we want our kids to take responsibility for their behavior, then we have to give them responsibilities along with guidance and support and love.

But they also have to be making decisions that matter. I often hear teachers talk about how they give kids the chance to choose when the teachers don't really care about the outcome and, of course, that's nothing close to a democratic classroom. The kids have to be able to make decisions when it matters very much to the teacher because that's authentic choice.

There are examples all over the place of what I call pseudo-choice where they have to make the so-called right decision or it doesn't count or it's these awful attempts to coerce kids that are wrapped in the language of choice, such as "Would you like to finish your homework now or do it after school?" This is not a choice at all, of course. It's saying to the kid, "Do what I tell you or I'll punish you," and this is a staple of many disciplinary programs. We help kids make good choices by making sure they are informed about the options they have and also that the options are appealing. A kid who gets to choose between two workbooks or silly essay questions or the time of day in which to memorize math facts is not being offered real choice. Somewhere Shakespeare says there is little choice in rotten apples.

Q: When teachers tell you they are offering choice in the classroom, do you find what some of them describe is superficial choice rather than real choice?

A: Many times, yes. Many times. In fact, even the major vehicle by which students can choose together, the class meeting, turns out to be a charade in many classes. First of all, it is often not used at all in secondary schools. Give elementary teachers credit for at least trying this kind of thing. Everybody gets to get in a circle on a regular basis, to reflect and plan and decide; but in many classes where the teachers are proud of themselves for doing this, they are running the whole show. They are asking or answering every question and driving the agenda and rarely trying to bring the students in on what they had already decided has to happen and that's hardly worthy of the name "choice."

I witnessed one class meeting where — I still shudder thinking about it — where every child in the room was to say something good and bad that had happened that week, and most of the bad stories had to do with one little boy named Charles. It became in effect an Orwellian hate session focused on this boy, and instead of intervening, the teacher underlined each comment by adding her own criticism addressed to the boy who had this eerie, blank expression the whole time.

Had you asked the teacher, she would have said, "Yes, we do class meetings, or we work on community in our classroom." But there was nothing worthy of the term *community-building* in what she modeled to the other kids, much less what she did to that one little boy.

Q: Have you talked to teachers who are struggling with this with positive results?

A: Yes, absolutely. That's where I've learned most of what's going on in my thinking. It's the practical realities in classrooms around the country that I've witnessed that animate my work and inform it. When I walk into a second-grade classroom in St. Louis and watch the kids running their own class meetings to solve problems that have come up, where one child is the facilitator and another is the recorder, thus teaching language skills, and the teacher is just sprawled out on the floor with the rest of them as they maintain a discipline, a patience, and a respect that would have blown me away if they were 17 but they were in fact seven years old. Or the story of a teacher in California who came back from her break to find the kids already huddled together excitedly talking about something, even though recess wasn't over, and when she asked what was going on was told a problem had happened during recess and they were holding a meeting to fix it by themselves. The kids didn't get there right away. In both those examples and many others I could share, what I'm really looking at is the hard work of the teacher in helping them to become empowered, to take responsibility not only for their own behavior but for the actions and values and feelings of everyone else as well as learning the skills of how to make decisions together.

For heaven's sake, most books and classes to which teachers are exposed take it for granted that the teacher must be in control of the classroom; and the only question is how you get and keep that control most effectively. What I want to call into question is the idea that the teacher ought to be in unilateral control of what's going on. I didn't question that premise when I was teaching. I never saw a classroom where a group of learners democratically figured out what the course ought to be, what to learn, how to learn, why to learn, how to treat each other, how they wanted to solve problems. I'd never read about or seen it, so my classrooms reflected my own experience. I imagine that's true for millions of teachers around the country. It's all the more remarkable, then, when you come across an example of somebody who miraculously has figured out that kids have to be active learners and that the best teaching is not where the teacher is most firmly in charge.

One caution must be mentioned — a perplexity with Deweyan-progressive teaching methods that goes back to many "progressive" schools of the 1920s and 1930s. This misunderstanding hinges on a reluctance — a guilty feeling even — to give necessary direction to what the students do when direction is needed. As one teacher wrote, "I felt [that] … it is okay to slip in a few ideas of your own and lead the kids a little to get a good project going." Of course it is! Students at almost any level (including graduate school) need teacher guidance and suggestions at times when they are learning to learn in a more independent and responsible way that is at variance with their previous school experience.

The teacher must always be the one who is responsible for the educational worth of a thematic unit or any other experience in the classroom. She knows more; she is mature; she is the one who, as Dewey writes, can see where the students' partial and less formed present knowledge might be directed (see Principle 18). The students can do most or some of this, but the teacher should have no hesitation to offer ideas, direction, and structure to make a faltering activity more educationally worthy. Students are learners who may be becoming more self-reliant and socially responsible, but when they need help, give it! That is what the office of teacher requires. If you are teaching thoughtfully, you need not worry that you will consistently over-direct or control as too many teachers do who subscribe to a more traditional teaching theory.

Dewey says, for example, in *Experience and Education* (1938), that "guidance given by the teacher to the exercise of the pupils' intelligence is an aid to freedom, not a restriction upon it" (pp. 84-85). This slim volume is well worth reading and discussing if a group of teachers is beginning to explore the educational moors where challenging progressive practice and seminal ideas push and shape each other.

PRINCIPLE 3

EVERY GREAT TEACHER
UNDERSTANDS THAT HE/SHE CANNOT
AFFORD TO UNDERESTIMATE WHAT IS
INVOLVED IN "KNOWING SOMETHING" WELL.

What does it mean to know history, or to be able to read? It must mean more than a grade or a standardized test score — yet, this is often the working definition schools give to these complex and potentially rich experiences. To "know" means active *thinking* in the sense that *more is learned than taught*. It means going beyond what is given. (See Dewey 1944, chaps. 11 and 12; Gardner 1991; Mitchell 1987; Newmann 1990a, 1990b; Perkins 1992).

Certainly knowing of some kind occurs at the level of factual recall or routine operations; however, if the teacher wishes to release potential in students, to promote individual growth, recall is not enough. Until learners are challenged to elaborate on what the world presents to them through their senses, they perpetuate an inadequate understanding of their own capabilities, contenting themselves with the naming, only, of what is presented. A hundred years ago William James wrote about the "going beyond": "But when we know about [something], we do more than merely have it; we seem, as we think over its relations, to subject it to a sort of treatment and to operate upon it with our thought" (1992/1890, p. 144). And if we who teach do not enable the elaborating, the going beyond what is given, we assume some of the guilt for the resulting inadequate self-understanding in students.

We can convey the spirit of what is involved in knowing by citing Jerome Bruner's (1966, 103-104) recollection of a notable event in his student days:

> We have all discovered [the active enterprise of reading], with delight, on our own. As a student, I took a course with I.A. Richards, a beautiful man and a great necromancer. It began with that extraordinary teacher turning his back to the class and writing on the blackboard in his sharply angular hand the lines [from Goethe's *Faust*]: "Gray is all theory; Green grows the golden tree of life."

For three weeks we stayed with the lines, with the imagery of the Classic and Romantic views, with the critics who had sought to explore the two ways of life; we became involved in reading a related but bad play of Goethe's, *Torquato Tasso*, always in a state of dialogue though Richards alone spoke. The reading time for eleven words was three weeks. It was the antithesis of just "reading," and the reward in the end was that I owned outright, free and clear, eleven words. A good bargain. Never before had I read with such a lively sense of conjecture, like a speaker and not a listener, or like a writer and not a reader.

One practical way for teachers to not underestimate what is involved in knowing a thing, is to observe and talk with their students as much as possible. In the example that follows, Ms. Shelly Salaman, Warminster, Pennsylvania, reveals Howard's process of thinking as he writes an essay on a topic he has chosen. This example leaves no doubt about many details involved in Howard's "knowing a thing": writing an essay on living in the country. Howard's story reveals, too, how thinking and feelings occur simultaneously in thought. Notice, for example, the strong feelings Howard has toward owning the future house he is writing about.

This interview between Howard and his teacher was tape recorded. Howard has some difficulty with learning and wisely (we think) refused placement in a special education class. Instead he was placed in classes of average ability with on-demand help as needed.

My House in the Country

Teacher: Is there anything you'd particularly like to write about, Howard? I'd like you to pick the topic.

Howard *[After a short pause]*: Living out in the country.

Teacher: Fine. Now, what I'd like you to do is just tell me aloud whatever goes through your mind as you work on this assignment.

Howard: [*Immediately*] Future — where I want to live — who with — married or something — I am going to build my own house — environment — surrounded by trees, all in back-yard, mountains, lake — then I wake up.

Teacher: You mean you come back to reality? [*laughter*]

Howard: Dune buggy, horse, animals, pets — what type of people? — transportation — I said that already — schools — what do you call it, shopping centers — how is the community about you? That's about it. [*Pause of about one minute*]

Teacher: It seems to me that what you've done is to freely associate ideas which are connected to the topic you chose. Is this the way you usually begin a writing assignment?

Howard: Yes, I get it all together.

Teacher: What is your next step?

Howard: I write it.

Teacher: Well, go to it. [*Howard writes for three minutes steadily; then he seemed to be reading his writing back to himself*] What are you doing now?

Howard: Reading it back, making sure I put down every word I said, checking for spelling, thinking what is next.

[*He went on reading another minute but made no changes. Next he wrote for about two more minutes; reread for about one minute and made a change on the seventh line of the rough draft*]

Teacher: Why did you make that change?

Howard: I wrote it backwards. I change something because I can add words and make a different meaning — spelling, if I can see it; my spelling is so bad. For example, I want to build my house and I added "own" [*said with great forcefulness*] because it's mine and means a lot to me.

Teacher: Yes, I can tell you feel strongly about the house. I bet you'll get it one day. [*Howard went on writing for about two minutes.*]

Howard: I'm reading the last sentence and maybe this is the ending. Or should I just leave it? [*Rereads, "mouthing" to self for about five minutes; he puts a period in.*] I don't know if I should write more or stop. I think I'm out of thoughts. [*Adds final words, "and then I woke up."*] I had a thought.

Teacher: Let me look at it.

Howard: [*Anxiously*] I'd normally write a rough copy and then reword it, change sentences around, add words, take them out — like right here: "I would like to live out in the country where the air is fresh ... ," I would change it and write "because" in there.

Teacher: Well, do that.

Howard: I'll probably add stuff.

Teacher: Great!

Interview held one day after the original writing session

Teacher: Howard, I was very pleased with the results of your writing, because I think it is the best writing you've ever done for me. Why do you think it was so good — so much better than other things you've done?

Howard: It was the topic. I've thought about it a lot, and I had a lot to say on it.

Teacher: I especially liked your first draft. Do you remember what you did or thought about as you changed your rough draft?

Howard: I reread it, adding words, changing words and sentences around to say what I wanted. Normally when I write, I leave out words — endings — my tutor told me that — same as when I read — I go back and try to put them in. That's why I do better orally in tests. In junior high a few of my teachers let me take tests orally.

Teacher: Do you still do that?

Howard: No, I don't need to do that now. I'm doing O.K. in my courses.

Teacher: How do you see yourself as a student?

Howard: I do well — I get mostly "B's" and some "C's" — but I know I need help with my writing and spelling.

Teacher: How do you feel about yourself as a writer?

Howard: The way I feel about writing is not too good because I can't write all the words I say and feel.

Teacher: Do you think you have any strengths and weaknesses?

Howard: My strong parts are that I can think of a lot to write about, but I can't write it down. My weakness is spelling.

Teacher: How do your teachers make you feel about your writing? Do they help you or make you feel worse?

Howard: I have five teachers. Four out of the five help me because I can always ask them questions about what's going on. I like all my teachers and most of them know I have a problem in reading and spelling.

Teacher: Was there anything any teacher has done that's been particularly helpful with your writing?

Howard: Yes, in 6th grade a teacher helped me. I stayed after school one day and she told me to use these questions — Who, What, When, Where, Why, and How, and they really help.

Teacher: Did that help you yesterday?

Howard: Yes, it told me how — how I wanted to live — and that's what I wrote about; and where, and when, in the future, and why.

Teacher: Let's talk specifically about your writing now. How do you go about writing?

Howard: First, I think of what I'm going to write and I say to myself, What am I going to say? [*pause*]

Teacher: Yes, I could see you doing that yesterday. It seemed to me that you followed a process of free association where you just let ideas happen, one triggering the next one.

Howard: Yes, I guess that's it.

Teacher: Look, let me show you the tape transcript. [*Shows him the transcript.*] See where you went from the word "future" to "where I want to live," to "who with" and so on, then to "dune buggy," "horse," "animals," "pets." That's a good process, Howard, to just let your thoughts flow.

Howard: Well, good.

Teacher: What do you do next, after the thinking?

Howard: Next, I write it. I'll write what I thought and reread it, and then go on — rereading helps me to figure out what to say, and I keep doing that — rereading to decide what to say — to put in words I missed....

Teacher: You know, Howard, one of the reasons I was so excited with yesterday's results is that you followed the same process that authors on writing recommend as being helpful.

Howard: Oh?

Teacher: Yes. There was planning or thinking like we just talked about, and then the writing of a rough draft with lots of rereading backwards for checking and more planning and thinking, and then there was final revision stage....

Howard: But what about my spelling?

Teacher: I have a book for that. I'll show it to you. [*Gives Howard a book for remedial students based on linguistic patterns.*] Let's get back to the writing process. Do you follow the same process I saw yesterday in your writing-up of class assignments?

Howard: No, I don't have time, and I'm not always as interested in the topic as yesterday.

Teacher: Well, I agree that interest is important. I couldn't agree more; but you can't always pick the topic in school. Still, there is something else you can do: Try to get to know as much about the topic as possible.

Howard: Thanks.

Teacher: Now, what I have to offer you in the way of help is this. If you really want to improve your writing, I'm going to demand from now on that at least one part of each of your papers for me be written with your best efforts, and I think following the right process, the one you followed yesterday, will make a big difference. I think I've been too easy on you in the past, but I'm going to demand more now.

Howard: [*Laughing*] Thanks a lot!

Schools are such busy places that "doing" teaching or administering become ends in themselves. We rarely stop the clock, step back, and try to see what we as teachers or administrators are doing. Only a few of us can observe our "Howards" carefully to see what they may be thinking or feeling.

Since we do not try to look critically at ourselves or our students too often, learning/teaching routines become part of the school's woodwork, where they lurk unseen to work their "will" for good or mediocre ends.

Fred Newmann's (1990a, 1990b) extensive work in high school social studies classes on "going beyond what is given" is a good empirical statement of what this criterion can mean. Newmann maintains that the "defining feature of higher order thinking ... is tasks or questions that pose cognitive challenge and require students to go beyond the information given" (1990b, p. 256). In his studies, six minimal criteria assumed to constitute "thoughtfulness" were developed from extensive classroom observation: (1) "Sustained examination of a few topics rather than superficial coverage of many"; (2) "Substantive coherence and continuity"; (3) "Students were given an appropriate amount of time to think and to respond"; (4) "The teacher asked challenging questions or structured challenging tasks"; (5) "The teacher was a model of thoughtfulness"; (6) "Students offered explanations and reasons for their conclusions" (1990b, p. 257).

Teachers who attend to these features of classroom interaction will increase their chances of not underestimating what is involved in "knowing something" well.

PRINCIPLE 4

EVERY GREAT TEACHER REALIZES THAT
PRODUCTIVE EXPERIENCE RESULTS FROM
DOING SOMETHING WITH FORESIGHT,
WITH PURPOSE IN MIND,
THEN REFLECTING ON THE CONSEQUENCES.

This principle captures the essence of thinking in real life. We are faced with a problem whose solution is unclear, for example, or we are engaged in a routine activity such as driving, when new elements enter the routine situation and confound it. Most of us use foresight when we drive and do think of the possible consequences of our actions. (If we did not do this, many of us would have long ago passed on!)

Teacher Estelle is driving home from school. But there is more to the driving situation than "driving home." Estelle is to pick up her daughter downtown. Estelle is a few minutes late. She drives faster. Her worry grows. She is further delayed by road construction. She is now fifteen minutes late. The psychological pressure mounts. Estelle is behind a slow-moving car as they approach a long curve. She cannot see far enough down the road to be certain that she can safely pass the car; on the other hand, she probably could make it. Feelings fight with judgment. Anxiety about her child says, "Pass. Take a chance." Because Estelle is a thoughtful person, she resists the pressure of her emotions and foresees the consequences of a risky driving decision: a possible head-on accident, injury, even death. This thinking process somehow relaxes Estelle. Being late to pick up her daughter has fewer bad consequences (although there are some) than the closer and more likely consequences of a risky driving decision that may save only a minute but take a life.

This illustration is unremarkable in itself, even obvious. "Obviousness" is one characteristic of doing some things with foresight. We do it routinely in many situations and are, therefore, oblivious to the thinking process involved. But there is an elusive quality in doing something with foresight, and in evaluating the goodness or badness of the consequences that follow the action. The elusiveness of foresight is dominant in too much teaching. Teacher Estelle, in other words, may be a thinking wizard behind the wheel of her Ford Escort, but in class she may see few consequences to children of her actions; she lacks foresight because she does not link her actions with their consequences — what her actions "bring out" in the complexity of a classroom. Sometimes whole school faculties are blind to the consequences of their actions to themselves and students as the following anecdote makes clear.

How Two Elementary Schools Became Entangled in a Web of Unforeseen Consequences

The principal author is in the third year of a five- to eight-year reform effort with seven schools in a middle-class school district enrolling 3,500 students. All of the administrators and about 60 percent of the teachers are engaged in a dialogue process in which the participants bring their practical knowledge to bear on some classical readings in history and educational theory. Presently (1994) each of the school dialogue groups is moving to practical action in reform through the development of school "action plans" while direct attention to the readings and their discussion is reduced. The school action plans, in short, reflect whatever influence the readings and discussion have had on the teachers' and principals' real-life theory of education. The action plans are always tentative.

So much for background. We share now the revealing events in two elementary schools that show the blindness of the collective faculty to the consequences of its actions until conversation in the dialogue yanked off the cover under which those consequences had been hiding for years.

The topic for the session was the practical implications, if any, of Lawrence Cremin's history, *The Transformation of the School*, for them as teachers and for their action plan. Cremin's book tells about the people, ideas, and events that shaped the progressive education movement. Someone mentioned Francis Parker's work in the 1870s that anticipated the whole language movement (Parker's students wrote much of the material they read) and today's "outcome-based" education movement. This led to a discussion of thematic units and the integration of subject matter around rich themes or topics. One subject that fits nicely into most thematic units is art. The art teacher saw a problem with that and said to the moderator something like, "You said an art teacher could spend two hours over several days or more working with teachers and their classes. I can't do that. I have to give every teacher in this building one-half hour or so on a regular schedule. I have to see everyone. I can't miss anyone." When asked why she thought this was true, she replied that the union contract demanded it. Hold this situation in your mind while we visit another elementary school one week later whose teachers were discussing Cremin's book in relation to their action plans.

In the second elementary school the teachers talked about thematic units, portfolios, and authentic assessment, among other topics. The question of time for teachers to plan came up as it had before. This led to a discussion of how often teachers in self-contained classrooms were disturbed by kids being pulled out of class for such things as speech correction, remedial work, gifted work, music, guidance. The teachers' comments made it clear that the self-contained classroom was in shreds. The moderator asked one teacher who was known to be a superb teacher how many hours each week she had her class intact. "Oh! About one hour," she calmly replied. No teacher seriously differed with her statement.

What do these abbreviated vignettes have to do with foresight and consequences of which Principle 4 speaks? Over a period of at least ten years, actions had been taken by the central administration (which preceded the current one) to add specialized programs from self-esteem lessons to speech to art to Chapter 1 classes in a helter-skelter manner unguided by an explicit, coherent theory of education. The principals never questioned this because, for example, lessons in self-esteem seemed like a good idea, and they, too, had no clear philosophy to guide them. The teachers, likewise, went along with each little added piece that did not seem to be bad in itself until today, years later, the teachers have lost much control over how time is used in their supposedly self-contained classrooms!

Elementary schools willy-nilly shaped themselves on the worst features of most middle and high schools. Art teachers are not certain that they can work in thematic units, and the classroom teachers are beginning to realize that they have lost one of their most valuable educational assets: virtually a whole day every day with the same group of kids. What harmful consequences of mindless acts!

Today these elementary schools are relatively time- and schedule-bound to the detriment of students and teachers alike. Teaching and learning has been made more difficult than need be. The future will tell whether or not these teachers and their principals can reform their shredded day into a more coherent whole.

What could be further from cultivating thinking in the minds of many of us than the *educational connections* that might be made between five seemingly unrelated elements: school buses, discipline problems on the buses, conversation, homerooms and the bus drivers themselves? Ms. Sybil Gilmar, then a vice principal at the Welsh Valley Middle School, Lower Merion, Pennsylvania, gives us a shining example of thinking within one's ordinary experience.

Thinking and the School Bus Problem

I found myself wasting a lot of time on student misconduct on the bus. The misconduct reports dealt with such things as noise level, disobeying the driver, and squabbles over who sat where. Do you know that each hat tossed out a school bus window costs about three hours in administrator and secretarial time? This is the kind of thing that I didn't want to dedicate my life to, although the safety implications of some of this behavior were potentially serious.

What to do about these endless reports? How could I avoid wasting time on educationally trivial matters, and still deal with the problem?

I decided to put the social responsibility idea of Dewey's to work. I created a dialogue among students, staff, and bus drivers. I began by asking students to respond to a survey that asked four open-ended questions about riding on the school bus.

1. The thing I dislike most about riding the school bus is…

2. The thing I like best about riding the school bus is…

3. Students can help to make a ride safe and pleasant by…

4. Bus drivers can help to make a ride safe and pleasant by...

Before these questions were given to the students, I discussed concerns about the buses with the teachers, and asked if they would run the survey in homerooms or in other classrooms. Mr. Brubaker, our principal, met three times with the bus drivers to discuss the survey results.

The survey summary is given below. Two of the results that later events proved to be important were the students' feeling that they liked bus drivers who were firm and friendly; the major concern of bus drivers was that they were often treated with disrespect by the students.

1. Major complaints were overcrowding, saving seats, picking on younger and smaller students, and the noise level.

2. One of the things students like about the bus is meeting their friends and socializing. A large number of students also appreciate getting a ride to school.

3. Most students understand what constitutes a safe and pleasant ride. They also understand the rules: (a) stay seated; (b) use a quiet voice; (c) line up without butting and pushing.

4. Students respected bus drivers who were firm but fair; that is, who did not allow "mayhem" and were also friendly to the students. Bus drivers, in turn, would like respect from the students. Some feel that they have a job that is not appreciated by the community.

5. Since school started in September, there have been 47 detentions for bus misconducts, one student has been denied bus privileges for a week, and one student was suspended from school for two days for inappropriate behavior on the bus.

The questions for discussion in the 26 homerooms are given below:

1. What's the best way to avoid being picked on?

2. What do you see as your role if you see someone being picked on?

3. What's the best way to get a seat if someone is "hogging" and even intimidating students?

4. How can the noise level be reduced, especially in light of the fact that students want to talk and see friends?

5. How can we raise the level of respect for bus drivers?

Although the survey aroused some interest, my main idea was that the dialogue in 26 homerooms, built around the discussion questions, might be the thing I wanted to raise the students' consciousness of the problem. The student/teacher dialogue was held during the guidance period.

The teachers reported the major feelings and ideas expressed by students in their homeroom discussions during a faculty meeting. All students saw the film, "And Then It Happened," the point of which is that misconduct can lead to a bus accident.

One of the major outcomes of the dialogue was that kids want bus drivers to be friendly — to say "Hello" and to know the children's names. This is one aspect of the respect desired by the drivers. Both the students and the drivers were aware of the suggestions and concerns of the other group.

The results of our talking were beyond anything we had hoped for. *Four months after our exchange of views, bus misconduct reports had dropped over 50 percent,* slightly higher than the drop that occurred immediately following the student-teacher-bus driver dialogue.

Dewey's idea that learning is problem-solving in which individual experiences are shared with others through the give-and-take of thoughtful talk worked well on the mundane problem of bus discipline. Both the students and the bus drivers "re-connected" in a socially positive way.

More rules and more detentions pushed from my office would only have increased the trivial element in my work. It is doubtful that such actions would have brought results comparable to that achieved by open conversations.

Ms. Gilmar's story not only shows how smart teachers can use in-school social situations as powerful civic content, but demonstrates as well Dewey's dictum that the worth of an idea acted upon can best be determined from the consequences that flow from that act. The 50 percent drop in bus misconduct reports is one indication that the homeroom dialogues (an action) by Ms. Gilmar led to desirable consequences.

PRINCIPLE 5

EVERY GREAT TEACHER RECOGNIZES THAT THINKING IS NOT SEPARATED FROM DOING SOMETHING WITH A PURPOSE IN MIND; THAT MIND IS IN THE DOING, NOT OUTSIDE IT.

In schools we find from time to time a needless division of experience into two worlds — ideas and practical affairs. That separation impoverishes both ideas and practice since ideas have meaning only within the continuous experience, that is, the practical life, of the individual or the larger social group (classroom, school, school district, state, nation, and beyond); and, conversely, practical life is meaningless unless informed by ideas. It is as if we have not learned to trust ourselves or our students to *think*.

The truth is, thinking comes dressed in the most ordinary of clothes, the clothes of day-to-day life experience. It is uncomfortable with the dress schools often drape on its figure, a fashion that often mimics a scarecrow. Thinking is not in tests; thinking is not in grades; thinking surely is not in dry, *Reader's Digest*-like textbooks that give a black-and-white sketch of history or literature, yet pretend to present the subject in living color.

Thinking is common, yet elusive. The teacher in the example of Principle 3 who carefully studied Howard's way of writing was thinking and not merely "assessing for a grade"; the elementary teachers who seem to have lost control over their self-contained classrooms discussed in Principle 4 are beginning to think after a decade-long "blackout" in which the cumulative consequences of many isolated actions in adding programs to the schools seems to have lowered, not raised, the quality of the schools for students.

This principle places thinking in *activity*, trying to do something the outcome of which is in doubt, uncertain, problematic. Reread the principle. It implies that inquiring is primary; acquiring is secondary. The short first phrase means that the process of trying to solve some problem, or doing something socially complex like raising a child, or restoring a car — the *activity* itself that requires *thinking* (i.e., inquiry) — is the essential thing. The second phrase means that in a true activity of thinking, one "picks up" (i.e., acquires) facts and values that, combined with thoughtful doing, enable one to construct personal and social knowledge. This is precisely what Frank Smith means when he notes that "knowledge is a byproduct of experience, and experience is what thinking makes possible" (1990, p. 12).

In thoughtful *doing* one learns persistence, discipline; in thoughtful doing one learns to appreciate the materials and people one works with in the activity, to appreciate the complexity and the quiet joy of doing something well, and depending on the range of activities over several years, a whole book of powerful learning could be compiled. If one thinks, according to Deweyan theory and to writers such as Smith, an almost unlimited range of learning occurs, much of which cannot be predicted beforehand by the teacher. Learning falls from thought as surely as the rain from clouds.

Greg Wegner (1990) of the University of Wisconsin at LaCrosse tells how family photographs can be used to encourage kids to "think history." The following is an excerpt from his article, "What is History?" (from the Spring 1990 issue of *Democracy & Education*) that views students as imaginative *makers* of history.

What is History?
Time, Imagination, and Creative Thinking
for Students as Makers of History

History is inherently controversial. What we think we know about history is rooted in conflicting interpretations about reality and the meaning of the past. The power to interpret, which speaks directly to the process dimension of history ... [encourages students] to build upon and go beyond memory-based learning into a higher level of thinking.

One of the legacies left to education by Mark Twain is the understanding that the young, through their innate creativity and imagination, have a natural affinity toward learning about the historical process through the all important lens of interpretation. Developing the power of interpreting the past demands the kind of classroom environment where students can discover, in various ways, that they are active agents in the historical process and that their own generation occupies a time frame in history. Each human being is thereby seen as a maker of history rather than a passive observer....

Photographs and Social History

One of the catalysts for attempting the difficult challenge of seeking some kind of union between content and process in the classroom came through a box of old family photographs at an estate auction that no one wanted.... The images subsequently found a special home in the classroom where they became the centerpiece for a lesson associating creative writing and thinking with the study of history.

What follows are a number of ideas on how photographic imagery, in this case family pictures, can be introduced into the history curriculum as a way of advancing the content and process dimensions of history....

The photographs could be introduced as part of a unit on "What is History?" during the first day or week of a history curriculum. One essential learning goal growing out of the activity is engaging students in the challenging prospect that the meaning of history cannot possibly be encompassed within the pages of a textbook. An understanding of history also involves a certain command of one's mother tongue. The written record of the past requires that people attach meaning or *interpretation* to historical evidence. It is at this point in the classroom that historical information becomes knowledge.

With unnamed and undated photographs in hand, students are asked to surmise the date the picture was taken and to provide clues from the photograph that might aid them as historians in this decision. The possibilities, depending on the collection, might range from clothing and hair styles to jewelry and the technology of the period necessary to produce the picture. The role of the students as "history detectives" might also extend to a discussion on why these people bothered to have these family portraits taken in the first place. It should be added that for most of us and our forebears, the only public documents marking the passing of a human life are found in family photographs, the obituary column of a newspaper, a death certificate, and a tombstone. The family pictures therefore represent part of the grist or raw material of social history.

To accentuate the importance of time frames and generations, students can focus on one historical personality in the photograph. After giving a first and last name to that individual, the class can then make a judgment on the year the person was born as well as the possible date of death. Such an activity will reinforce the fact that the person pictured occupied a time frame in history and was an active participant in the historical process. One related exercise that could be introduced at this point is the discussion of possible changes in American or world history which took place during or since the lifetime of the person in the picture. By not giving the actual date of the photograph at the outset, even if it is available, students can actively use their historical imaginations and knowledge about history.

As a corollary to Twain's insistence that children make their own historical pictures, it is suggested here that students *write* their own historical interpretation as a way of attaching meaning to the historical lives of people in the old photographs. Taking an example out of E. L. Masters' *Spoon River Anthology*, students can write an essay from their own historical imaginations about the daily life experienced by the subject of the picture. An exchange of student essays the following day might serve as the basis for a discussion of the similarities and contrasts of the life experiences of the personalities in the picture.

The importance of perception and its relationship to conflicting interpretations in the history among the young writers in the class is illustrated with even greater force if every student has been given a copy of the *same photograph* as a preliminary to this writing exercise. The clash of interpretations stemming from something as profound as what we actually "see" in the photograph can be related to the serious difficulty of interpreting the meaning of past personalities, developments, and events among historians. By exploring these considerations, students of history may come to the healthy notion that historical knowledge is not something that is poured from one standing brain to another in the form of dates and names stripped of historical context. On the contrary, the box of old photographs should leave investigators of the past with the conclusion that historical facts devoid of context and the acceptance of a consensus view of the meaning of the past do not mean "history" at all.

Extending Time and Imagination

Using the process orientation of history and the foundation created through the box of old family photographs, a number of other classroom activities can serve as additional points of departure.

Assume that the old box of family photographs included pictures of only white families. How might the essays written on "A Day in the Life of ..." be different if the people in the pictures were Black? Hispanic? Asian Americans? After conducting a search of photographs from their own family histories, students could take time to consider the conclusions they, as social historians a century from now, might draw concerning American culture using the pictures as evidence.

As a way of bringing the concepts of time, history, and imagination into sharper focus, one could consider the following problem: Is there anything from present-day American culture worthwhile enough to save for generations of human beings 3,000 years from now? What historical artifacts from American culture should be included in a time capsule which could give historians from that era an accurate picture about the society in which we live? What values should be represented? What artifacts, including photographs, in such a time capsule would symbolize those values? The preparations for the time capsule could include student essays describing American culture for future historians. Some of the topics can range from school culture to music, art, sports, death customs, and the influence of computers as well as other technological changes. Additional essays might advance a set of predictions describing the condition of human culture in the world at some time in the future.

The study of history can contribute to the mental health of young people. It has this potential when it advances critical thinking about the nature of what it means to be a mortal human being and an active member of the body politic. This contribution is further reinforced when members of the younger generation in classrooms are given the challenge to think about the profound notion that they occupy their own time frame in history and are in their own right active participants in the historical process. Time and imagination, concepts central to the legacy left by Mark Twain and Edgar Lee Masters, are critical for this kind of history teaching.

Mr. Wegner has shown us one practical way to encourage students and teachers to "think history."

Teaching Objectives

PRINCIPLE 6

EVERY GREAT TEACHER KNOWS THAT
LEARNING OBJECTIVES SUGGEST THE KIND
OF ENVIRONMENT NEEDED TO INCREASE
THE CAPACITIES OF THE LEARNER.

The spirit of this principle is most directly illustrated by reflecting on two alternative objectives, both of which many teachers would endorse. One objective might be stated this way: "Sixth-grade students are expected to score at or above grade level in social studies on the 'Bull's Eye' standardized test." The second objective is stated as follows: "Sixth-grade students are expected to learn social studies and literature content in small groups by the beginning of the spring semester."

To simplify this explanation, assume two conditions to be true: (1) that the teachers will act on one or the other of these objectives in class — the objectives are not window dressing; and (2) that one of these objectives is the only one that the sixth-grade classes in an imaginary school will try to meet this year.

The objective related to the Bull's Eye standardized test scores might reasonably suggest a classroom and school environment marked by the following qualities:

- Textbooks and workbooks will be the primary materials for learning because they are readily available, they cover the content to be tested, and they are judged to be efficient.

- Facts in social studies will be emphasized over concepts because the test involves fact recall.

- Social studies content that differs from that on the test may not be taught if time pressures are great or if the school is publicly ranked with other schools on the basis of standardized test scores.

- Instruction will be didactic: pupils will read the book, listen to the teacher's elaboration of the text, and take the chapter quizzes.

Allowing for the possibility of many other (perhaps better, perhaps worse) responses to this objective, the learning/teaching environment suggested by these qualities might well have these characteristics:

- The teacher is active, the students more passive.

- The teacher/student talk in the classroom is dominated by the teacher 70% or more of the time (Goodlad 1984; Hillocks 1989). Most student talk will be in the form of short-answer responses to the teacher. This limits the amount of student talk which directly lowers the intellectual quality of the learning. Most talk will take place within the total class group.

- Trade books, such as biographies or historically-based fictional accounts of life in the colonial period, for example, are less likely to be used to supplement the text material.

- Writing experiences for the pupils may not be perceived as relevant to the test or to learning the content. Responses in workbooks or on dittoed sheets take precedence.

- Art or music activities are not thought to be substantively or motivationally related to social studies because they take time away from the "content" to be covered and tested.

So we see how an objective with certain characteristics limits the quality of the learning environment, depending on the individual and collective response of teachers. The environment developed here in response to a standardized test objective responds to the limited objective, which shows how poor objectives can drain the intellectual and social vitality from a classroom or school.

The idea connoted by Principle 6 is not to hold ourselves to a too-demanding standard that practical circumstances might well proscribe, but rather to squeeze the best learning environment possible from whatever real constraints exist. We *are* accountable for thinking and for trying things out. We *are not* responsible for achieving perfection removed from the conditions of practice.

The second objective for the imaginary 6th-grade class, to work constructively in small groups, suggests such qualities as the following:

- School is a place in which both individual and cooperative work is valued.

- Student learning activities do not have to be continuously directed nor controlled by the teacher. A social situation itself, properly set up over time, can exert a disciplinary influence.

- Group work can allow students of differing talents and abilities to succeed. This opportunity offers an alternative to dependence on total class instruction. It also opens up new avenues for student success, provides a task-oriented situation for useful talk and activity, and provides students with a chance to plan, to talk, to write, to read and discuss, or to construct something that has purpose and intellectual value.

- Students can be taught gradually to work under general teacher supervision if learning to work in groups is perceived as a complex activity in which certain skills and attitudes necessary for its success are taught.

- Students can help each other to learn by sharing responsibilities to achieve a common goal.

It is reasonable to assume that the classroom environment suggested by this objective would help to develop capacities in pupils to become more independent in their learning; to share work and responsibility among peers; to plan, organize, and execute some program or event; and to learn the persuasive, social, and political skills needed to accomplish a purpose requiring mutual sustained thought and effort. The open quality of the second objective is its strength — in the hands of good teachers; in the hands of poor teachers, its openness becomes a weakness.

The two objectives that illustrate Principle 6 suggest two very different learning environments. Each environment values certain things to be learned, and each will lead to different teacher and student behaviors and learning outcomes. Those who say that an objective is merely a clear target and all that counts is hitting it forget that to "hit it" certain *means* must be chosen. The means alter elements of the classroom environment and exert an educational influence in their own right. The quality of the *means* chosen to reach an objective may be educationally more important than the objective itself, once the latter has been chosen and judged to be desirable. This idea leads us to the next principle.

PRINCIPLE 7

EVERY GREAT TEACHER KNOWS THAT THE OBJECTIVES VALUE BOTH WHAT IS TO BE LEARNED AND HOW IT IS TO BE LEARNED. THE QUALITY OF LEARNING IS CRITICALLY DEPENDENT ON HOW THE OBJECTIVE IS ACHIEVED.

One learns both from the end achieved — the skill of adding, for example — and the process of learning itself. What one learns from the process of learning is usually implicit, subtle, below the level of conscious analysis. Processes used, however, strongly influence attitudes toward the subject, teacher, and school; they may help or hinder learner motivation. In fact, the learning processes typically used are the *primary* determinant of the *quality of the learning* (and consequently of the quality of any classroom, school, or school system).

The single most important source for improving the quality of education lies in the processes (means) used by the students, teachers, and administrators while they are learning, teaching, and leading. Any *single* "product" measure, such as standardized tests, behavioral objectives, or criterion-referenced tests, undervalues those processes. Tests alone are an insufficient base to answer questions like those posed by state legislatures and boards of education: How good are our schools? What are we getting for the millions of dollars we are spending?

One should not be intimidated by foolish talk about the measurability (often couched in the language of accountability) of school outcomes — as in "if it can't be measured, we can't know if anything good is occurring." Friendship cannot be quantitatively assessed; nor can loyalty, or love, or self-discipline, or ethical behavior, or initiative. Most of us, however, would call them "significant outcomes." Similarly, there are centrally important school goals that do not easily lend themselves to numerical ranking.

The essence of the idea behind the fundamental relationship between process and product is simple: The quality, good or poor, of any learning result (reading, say) lies in the quality of the processes used to reach it — "learning to read." As conceived by "practical" educators, objectives are qualitatively neutral, i.e., "This class will be on, or six months above, grade level by May 15." Once this objective, however limited, has been set, the only *proper* and *practical educational* concern should be a rigorous comparison and selection of the best qualitative means to get there.

Once the goals are established, the emphasis shifts to the processes used to reach them. Everything lines up behind the goals: the kinds of instructional materials used; the things kids, teachers, and principals do in school; the explicit and subtle qualities of classroom and school environment (its socio-psychological "feel"; its ethos); the kinds of student, teacher, principal, and school evaluation procedures that are used, and so on. The "lining-up" cannot be done rapidly — not even in a one-week "inservice" program! Under good conditions, coherence between means and ends is likely to be achieved slowly over years, not weeks or months.

Let's take an example at the senior high school level.

Processes Used to Achieve the Goal of Being Able to Write Standard English in Reports	
E. L. Thorndike School	Francis Parker School
Formal grammar is taught in a programmed text format.	Writing is integrated within a core block of English-Social Studies that meets eight hours per week.
Skill exercises in elements of writing (topic sentence, transitions, etc.) are completed.	Half of the work is built around periods of American history in which themes (child labor, unions, industrialization) are approached from the perspectives of literature and history.
Twice a month short papers are graded by the teacher and discussed in the total class setting.	Written work grows out of the theme work and involves experiences in peer group criticism and discussion of substantive English-Social Studies content.

Processes Used to Achieve the Goal of Being Able to Write Standard English in Reports	
E. L. Thorndike School	Francis Parker School
Grammar is taught separately from writing.	The teacher evaluates written work and shares the evaluation with the student. Occasional total class sessions on grammar are held as dictated by the written work; otherwise, grammar is taught as needed based on what a student writes.
Evaluation consists of completion of programmed text exercises, and changes in writing achievement are plotted on standardized tests required by the state.	Qualitative evaluation of the year's papers is done by each student and by small task groups; the teacher and students evaluate class processes; and standardized tests required by the state are administered.

Although the processes used by the Thorndike and the Parker schools are somewhat stereotypical, they will serve our purpose: to make more concrete the fundamental idea that educational *quality* is "built-in" by the processes used over weeks and months, and is not assessed simply by standardized test scores.

In general, Thorndike uses a more direct, "practical" approach: Grammar is taught as a separate skill indirectly related to writing; the subject is arranged in a logical, linear sequence by the programmed text; the process generally ignores factors such as integrating writing within larger "wholes" of experience; and writing is seen more as an end in itself rather than as a means to larger ends, such as creating and then sharing meaning. Parker, on the other hand, uses a meaningful process that embeds the writing in a larger "unit" and makes writing more functional and presumably more interesting. Small groups are used for peer teaching for both substantive content and writing process; they also provide a group context for oral and written communication.

This progressive and thoughtful process, in sum, provides a richer experience for all of the learner's work in English-Social Studies which should add depth to the learning. The process makes the learning more functional without detracting from its academic quality.

The evaluation of outcomes in the Parker school includes both product and process. The evaluation of the course process by both teachers and students reinforces the importance of the learning/teaching processes used and provides a valid data source from which to improve the course — at little or no cost. The qualitative assessment of written work by the teacher *asserts* the necessity for subjective, professional effort in evaluation, and recognizes that writing assessment is *inherently* subjective because of its complexity. Finally, as Calfee (1988) and Wiggins (1993) recommend, the locus of the evaluation is with those closest to the students, not in a test-construction factory miles away.

It would be reasonable to assume that although both schools teach to the target writing objective, the learning by students in the Parker school would be qualitatively superior because the means chosen to reach the objective are in themselves qualitatively superior to those of the Thorndike school.

Similarly, the teaching of science offers another way of viewing this dichotomy. Laboratory work may be used to explore questions so that the student will arrive at a solution through his or her inquiry. One school might provide laboratory work as a *verification* of what was learned in class and from the textbook. Another school might *open* the issue under investigation to a wide range of experiments. In the latter school, the solutions are unknown at the beginning of the experiment, and the student subsequently checks his or her conclusions against the established body of knowledge. Here again the two processes are qualitatively different and thereby have a different impact on the outcome.

Lynn Romney, a biology teacher at Vernal Jr. High (Utah), has a simple way to improve the "how" of learning for some students, according to Katherine Smith, a fellow teacher.

> Lynn carefully matches up students as lab and study partners. She makes sure that every student who is struggling has a partner capable of explaining labs and concepts, and then encourages cooperation. At the same time, she makes sure that the students have had a chance to learn every important concept through a variety of ways, and that students have an opportunity to pursue each topic in greater depth, according to interests and abilities.

In stark contrast to this approach, a biology department at a large high school in Salt Lake City is run in a unique fashion. Sharyle Karren, an intern in the principal's office at the time, tells the tale.

Kids in a Test Tube

The four biology teachers have their course pre-designed for them. Each teacher is expected to give the same lesson on the same day. The materials, worksheets, and guides are prepared ahead of time. When it is time for an examination, the department chair runs off the test and hands it out to the teachers on the very morning it is to be given so that the material does not get into "forbidden hands."

Each teacher complies with the pre-arranged curricular schedule and there are never any exceptions. As a consequence of the rigid sequencing of concepts, students are, in effect, "traded" back and forth among the teachers, according to who owes whom a favor and which teacher is tired of handling certain students in his or her class.

All students taking biology are expected to master the material at the same rate and under the same teaching style. As one could imagine, grading is an unpleasant reality: I know of a class in which 60% of the students received a "D" or an "F," one student received an "A," no student received a "B" and the rest received a "C"!

The pedagogical discrepancy between these two schools is staggering; yet, it is "biology" that is taught in both. Would anyone deny the validity of our claim that good objectives "reflect the understanding that the quality of learning is critically dependent on how that learning is achieved"? An interesting question that you may want to consider is, What realities might have led the high school department to adopt the sterile learning processes Karren describes above?

Finally, a mother, Lillian Zarndt, tells a poignant story of ends and means in an elementary art unit through a dialogue with her daughter.

Garbage Can Art

Elizabeth: Wow, Mom, look at those trees! They have eyes in them! (We are reading a book about a Caribbean legend, called *The Nutmeg Princess*. Elizabeth is in her pajamas; it's our good-night story.)

Mom: Yeah, I really love the artist's ideas. Look at this!

Elizabeth: It's a good thing my art teacher, Mrs. — , isn't seeing this! She'd make her throw it in the garbage and make her start over.

Mom: What do you mean? I don't understand.

Elizabeth: Well, when our pictures aren't what Mrs. ____ wants, we have to throw them in the garbage and start over. You know, the garbage can by the door. And besides, we get about three minutes to draw, and the rest of the time we're always cleaning up.

Mom: Really?

Elizabeth: Yup! And guess what. I was drawing this picture of white horses with golden hooves and the teacher said the hooves were too big and she made me throw it in the garbage and start all over again and it was just two minutes before the bell rang and then I couldn't finish my second picture and she always puts them away and then the next time I can't finish because I don't know where to find it. I think she has a closet somewhere.

Mom: Did you like your horse picture?

Elizabeth: It was sooo neat, Mom! I made the hooves really shiny and big because this was a magic horse that can fly and the hooves helped him fly and I could travel with him to places nobody knows about, just me.

Mom: Why did the teacher think the hooves were too big?

Elizabeth: Well I had to make them big because they were so important. How could the horse take off from the ground without big strong hoofs, huh?

Mom: I would love to see your white horse with golden hooves. Would you like to draw another one at home?

Elizabeth: Not really, Mom.

This story might help us understand that the quality of learning is determined by the quality of the processes used in the learning as Principle 7 suggests. It is sad when a student's best efforts end up as "garbage can art."

PRINCIPLE 8

EVERY GREAT TEACHER KNOWS THAT THE
IMMEDIATE CLASSROOM OBJECTIVES ARE
MADE WITH LARGER, OVERARCHING AIMS IN
MIND; THAT THEY FREE THE STUDENT
TO ATTAIN THE LARGER AIMS.

We teach reading in a limited setting so that students may read beyond those limits. This is obvious when stated in isolation from the flux of day-to-day school life; in practice, however, the point isn't all that clear. Consider that it was not until the 1970s that most Pennsylvania elementary schools had library collections of 8,000-10,000 books. Prior to that, it was apparent that teaching reading was implicitly viewed (insofar as the school was concerned) as an end in itself rather than as a means to wider learning.

Keeping one eye on this principle helps us to be less "teacherish," less myopic, less locked into immediate ends while forgetting ends beyond our classrooms. For example, the true end of teacher education is not ten semester credits at X university, but "good" teaching in Y town. The principle suggests that when we teach literature, for example, we ask, Does our teaching go *beyond* the teaching of literature? What proportion of our high school (or college) graduates voluntarily read literary works after graduation? If we knew the proportion, at what point would we become concerned that the objectives and processes of teaching literature may have become self-limiting, not "going beyond themselves"? Can our teaching be said to provide initiating experiences, or terminal experiences? If a high school or college graduate reads only *Time, People Magazine,* and *Cosmopolitan,* his or her whole education was indeed terminal in all senses of this scary word.

Literature is an area rich in possibilities for attending to this principle. If high school students study Camus' *The Stranger,* objectives beyond analysis and comprehension of the piece include interest in issues that emerge from it and extend beyond the school experience. For example, Is the death penalty an appropriate punishment for murder? This question itself is a stimulating source for an inquiry into the sensitive issue of how society protects itself from delinquent behavior. Other examples found in Camus' work are questions of personal integrity and the implications of compromising one's values.

Where Principle 8 speaks of "overarching aims" giving life to short-term objectives, instead of this more academic term we might have said, "a generous and humane vision." It is as true as it is unremarked by most educators that one's sense of life — how one sees its meaning and purpose — takes the clay of our intentions and makes something real of them. We ultimately teach what we are; we cannot escape the light and darkness in ourselves; it all comes out in the act of teaching or leading.

We share below the generous and humane vision of Terrance Furin, who, as superintendent of schools in the Owen J. Roberts School District, Pottstown, Pennsylvania, is bringing a moribund system to educational life. We can attest that the spirit of this lovely essay guides what Furin does when he works with groups of new teachers, with his board members, with teachers and principals in dialogue-based school reform, and with the "shop kids" who are too often written off by many of us who value a restricted view of the intellect much too highly. This piece first appeared in the Pottstown, PA, *Mercury* on September 23, 1992 (p. A8).

The Cathedral Within

Over the course of his career, Norman Cousins, editor of *The Saturday Review*, interviewed most of the world's influential people. In the course of these interviews, he usually asked the same question — "What is the most important thing you have learned in your lifetime?" The most moving response he received was from 1952 Nobel Peace Prize recipient Albert Schweitzer.

Schweitzer was a famous writer, musician, doctor, and missionary. Cousins went deep into what was then known as French Equatorial Africa to find Schweitzer, who was sharing his gifts of medicine with the native population. Over a meal one evening, Cousins asked his question. Schweitzer said that he would have to think about it and give his response at a later time. The next day Cousins awoke to find that Schweitzer had gone into a neighboring village to deliver a baby. After his return much later in the day, Schweitzer said that the most important thing he had learned in his lifetime was that each person contains a "cathedral within."

I was very moved when I heard Cousins tell his story at an educational convention several years ago. It has remained with me because the imagery of a "cathedral within" is so strong. It carries powerful implications for educational systems which are dominated by factory models of mass-production that have existed since the early 1900s.

Cathedrals are vast, complex, towering monuments to mankind's deepest yearnings and noblest aspirations. They are filled with intricate workmanship of awesome beauty containing masterworks of art and music. They are dedicated to celebrating the spiritual core of every being. Although containing many similarities, each cathedral is unique — as unique as each individual whose own cathedral embodies the unlimited grace of intelligence.

"Learning as the cultivation of intelligence" is the first of four design principles [that form] the basis of discussions for restructuring in the Owen J. Roberts School District. These discussions with teachers, administrators, students, parents, and citizens will take place over the next few years. They will sharpen the vision of the future, manifest the district's philosophy, and guide the growth of our schools. The cathedral of every person's special intelligence needs to be seen as something incredibly vast, complex, and spiritual. Such a conceptualization moves us beyond the behaviorist psychology common in the educational assembly-line emphasis on sameness — a sameness marked by uncritical memorization of encyclopedic facts.

Factory models of learning rely upon the teacher to provide "correct" information as a stimulus and the students to provide "uniform" responses. These models often break knowledge into small segments called behavioral objectives which are learned through repetitive drills. Learning seldom concentrates on higher thinking processes. Assessment is usually done through simple, machine-gradable, true-false or multiple-choice tests. Examples of sophisticated educational programs built upon these principles include Individually Prescribed Instruction (IPI), Individually Guided Education (IGE), and Mastery Learning. Other examples include reading systems which emphasize memorization of isolated rules and symbols outside of the texture and meaning of language, such as the Initial Teaching Alphabet (ITA) or a total phonics system. A basic assumption in these factory models is that general intelligence can be measured by mass tests based solely upon linguistic abilities. A different view of intelligence — and of education — is needed if American public schools are to progress beyond the factory model and prepare students for the different world of the 21st century.

Intelligence and learning need to be viewed in all of these vast complexities. Current psychologists, such as Howard Gardner, propose that the human mind is not one general intelligence but rather multiple intelligences. In his 1985 book, *Frames of Mind: A Theory of Multiple Intelligences,* Gardner develops the idea that there are essentially seven major intelligences: logical-mathematical, linguistic, musical, spatial, bodily-kinesthetic, interpersonal, intrapersonal. Schools need to recognize and develop each of these. This requires rich settings that provide for multiple differences. Intelligence has many faces, and the rote reciting of facts removed from ideas is not one of them.

One example of such a setting might be a study of the American Revolution which involves more than a memorization of chronological facts and examines alternative causes and effects based upon a hands-on study of actual historical documents. Such a study would emphasize economic, political, and social analyses and synthesize differing interpretations into a new evaluation developed by the student. Another example could be an integration of elementary art, music, and physical movement into a curriculum organized around various elements such as harmony, texture, color, and repetition.

Advocates of gifted education are well aware of the powerful possibilities which these and other examples hold for learning. What is true and good for gifted students is true and good for all students. Over the past two years, a group of students from Owen J. Roberts High School who were, for the most part, "turned off" to traditional schooling, has been involved in reading Nobel Prize authors, learning the history of Philadelphia through field experiences, and studying the ancient history of the Sumerians and Egyptians. On a recent visit to the University of Pennsylvania's Museum of Archaeology and Anthropology, one student said to another, "We're actually learning something today!" Amen.

If we are to take seriously the challenges facing our public school systems and if we hope to prepare our students for participation in the world of the next century, then we need to recognize that both intelligence and learning are extremely complex. We need to progress beyond the behaviorists' stimulus-response approaches and recognize that each person does contain a "cathedral within." Most of all, we need to help all students realize the beauty of each cathedral and act with reverence for the riches it contains.

> ### PRINCIPLE 9
>
> EVERY GREAT TEACHER KNOWS THAT MOST TEACHING OBJECTIVES OUGHT TO MAKE SENSE TO THE LEARNER AT THE TIME OF LEARNING AND THAT FUTURE LEARNING IS BUILT BEST ON WHAT THE STUDENT HAS ALREADY LEARNED.

Our theory permits no gaps in one's experience. Your life experience from birth to today looks like this:

Fig. 1. "Ups" and "downs," yes; but no gaps.
There was never a day in which you did not experience something.

Your life experience does not look like the sketch in Figure 2.

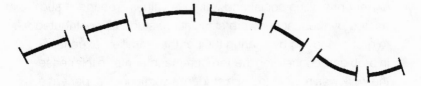

Fig. 2. Our life experiences are not disconnected from each other.

When you try to "teach" a student something, the new experience has to fit into that continuous life flow. Deficiencies in experience or knowledge cannot be filled by the teacher proposing something verbally, no matter how great the lesson plan. The lesson plan, in practical terms, can only enter at the "end" of the learner's "experience line" which occurs the moment before you teach. One's experience is continuous throughout life — not discontinuous. Life experience is like a wide river that a teacher must enter cautiously from the banks. Slowly a river will change over time, but it takes something as potent as the Army Corps of Engineers to make major changes in the river in a short time, often at great environmental cost. As a teacher you cannot, as can the engineers, change the student's "river of experience" quickly. You must know its flow and gently enter its water.

A recent Hebrew school class illustrates the point.

> The aim was to learn the Ten Commandments. It was obvious to the teacher that the Commandments, as they appear in the Bible, did not mean much to the students. Hence, the teacher undertook to view the intended learning from various perspectives which were significant to the students. The students worked in small groups on the following assignments provided to them by several teachers: give examples of each Commandment to explain its meaning; arrange them in priority according to our current social and religious values; according to your own beliefs, compare the Ten Commandments to the United States Constitution; and write your own ten commandments. The students compared their group activities and reflected upon the experience in discussion and drama.
>
> Although the students did not suggest this approach, it was of great interest to them because it fulfilled their needs. Their study was not of an isolated chapter in history, literature, or religion. Rather, it became meaningful through its relevance to current prevailing social and religious values. The ideas suggested by the teacher were stimulating; students contributed to group learning by sharing their or their families' experience in problems concerning the Ten Commandments. In this sense, the work was related to each student's continuous experience. Peer teaching, social interaction, mixing attitudes with skills and knowledge (not separating them), and showing (not telling) the significance of the subject matter to the child are all means a teacher can use to help pupils connect their present life with "today's" classroom goals.

This story suggests that even abstract content such as the Ten Commandments can sometimes be embraced by the students' previous experience if the teacher is imaginative enough to build a variety of "learning roads" that link the students' *past* experience to the *present* learning experience.

Subject Matter

Principle 10

Every Great Teacher Knows that Essential Content is Knowledge of General Social Significance that is Relevant to All Students, Whatever their Abilities or Interests.

Principle 11

Every Great Teacher Knows that Content Must Be Related to the Needs of the Local and Regional Community. It is Intended to Improve the Quality of Future Living for Both the Community and the Individual. Content Must Illuminate Significant Social Issues.

Principle 12

Every Great Teacher Knows that Content Does Not Consist Exclusively in Information or Data Readily Available in Books, Computers, or Other Media. Rather, Good Content is Subject Matter that Assists Learners in Their Inquiry and Their Attempt to Create Meaning.

These three propositions reinforce and build on each other in their focus on the content of subject matter. If subject matter is taught primarily as a study for specialists (as many courses from high school to college do), its significance for the broader social life is ignored. Science, for example, is typically treated in school from a technical perspective — as if science existed for its own sake. Where are the science courses that treat science as a liberal study, i.e., courses that consider what values underlie science, whether it is morally neutral, what its socially integrative and disintegrative influences are, and how it is related to technology?

Given undisputed facts about pollution of ground water in thousands of locations throughout the United States, for example, can we claim that chemistry is not also a *social* study? Given the problems of space exploration, can we say that physics, aeronautics, and space research are not also connected to social issues? We know, for example, something about earthly environmental pollution. What does that knowledge suggest about the possible pollution of space? Are we comfortable with cost estimates for space stations and military spy satellites that run to the scores of *billions* of dollars while lamenting the lack of human services for children or the homeless? And can we as a society fully confront such questions until we feel comfortable with our ability to understand them, instead of relegating them to the deliberations of biochemists, geneticists, and astrophysicists who alone, supposedly, are able to deal with such erudite topics?

In fact, the experts in too many cases have proven to be more of a bane than a boon to society. One commentator (Saul 1992) has depicted vividly the anti-social effects of technology run amok. He notes that "the experts are [not] held responsible for their own actions in any sensible manner because the fracturing of memory and understanding [in society generally] has created a profound chaos in the individual's sense of what responsibility is" (p. 17). School teachers and principals are in an enviable position to help society think sanely about the relationship between the technological and the social.

While it is true that as students mature, their ability to handle abstractions increases, teachers should not make the error of teaching as if content could be meaningfully divorced from present concerns and interests — something Principle 11 seeks to avoid. This idea suggests the importance of seeing uses for what is learned, and to be aware of how specific content relates to other pieces of content. John Holt (1964) observes: "A field of knowledge, whether it be math, English, history, science, music or whatever, is territory, and knowing it is not just a matter of knowing all the items in the territory, but of knowing how they relate to, compare with, and fit in with each other.... It is the difference between knowing the names of all the streets in a city and being able to get from any place, by any desired route, to any other place" (p. 106).

The subjects taught in schools, viewed from this larger perspective, would not primarily be seen as ends in themselves, or as something merely to be "learned" in the protective environment of the school removed from the larger social life.

With increasing amounts of information in all subject matters, you may feel a need to teach faster in order to "cover" as much material as you can, hoping that the information pumped into the learner's head will turn out somehow to be useful. Unfortunately, students cannot realistically use information that constitutes a basket of facts instead of coherent, meaningful knowledge.

In this connection, we should consider media and instructional aids provided by recent technology. Their apparent, even seductive, usefulness may lead us to provide them as a surrogate for teaching, rather than as an adjunct to it. They are so appealing and visually (or auditorily) dramatic that, without reflection, we may believe them capable of solving much of the problem of the information explosion. But, as Neil Postman (1992) points out in *Technopoly,* the attempt to relay information at greater and greater speeds and with greater and greater efficiency contributes to the *problem,* not to the solution. The problem is the *integration* and *coherence* of information, not its lack. Thus, subjecting the learner to multiple information transmitters does not necessarily serve as a base for understanding, applying, generalizing, analyzing, synthesizing — in other words, for creating personal meaning.

Rather than boring students with too many facts about World War II — the location of the Maginot Line, for example — one might instead focus on a "world-sized" idea, say the Holocaust, and have the students learn it by discovery. Probably every history book on the war mentions the terrible plight of the Jews. This string of words, likely emotion-free for many high school students today, can be given significant meaning as they start to inquire about the general issue of genocide (Indians in the United States in the 18th and 19th centuries, Armenians at the hands of the Turks in World War I, Kurds by the Iraqis in the 1960s and 1980s, and the Rwandan and the Serbian-Bosnian-Moslem horrors of the 1990s).

One could deal with the Holocaust from the standpoint of children and adolescents, using, for example, *Friedrich and I Was There* by Haris Peter Richter, *Night* by Elie Weisel, *I Never Saw A Butterfly* by H. Valavkova, and drawings and poetry by children in the Terezin concentration camp. Students could look for materials on the Holocaust with a focus on one aspect of the ordeal. They could be helped to express their knowledge, feelings, and impressions in writing, painting, discussion, or any other form.

Media (films, records, newspapers) *can* supplement classroom activities or initiate discussion of the topic, but they should not be allowed to take the place of inquiry. Basic problems, typically in the form of questions, must be explored: Why the Jews? What are sources of anti-Semitism? Why the Germans? Should the Jews have resisted more extensively? *Could* they have resisted more extensively? How is anti-Semitism connected to racism and prejudice in our society?

Have the students deal with real-world daily situations while they pursue their work: What happens if you disobey your parents or the law? If a person were being attacked physically, would you walk away, watch, call for help, or take steps to stop the fight?

Drama can play an important role in understanding the attitudes and behavior of the Germans, Jews, and other contemporaries. One could use literature about the Holocaust written by survivors (*Escape from Freedom* by Erich Fromm, *Man's Search for Meaning* by Viktor Frankl), literature about Nazi Germany (*The Tin Drum* by Gunter Grass, *Propaganda: The Art of Persuasion, WW II* by Anthony Rhodes), art created during the war, and contemporary documents to stimulate thinking, draw conclusions, and generalize ideas. Reflection on the Holocaust from the perspective of the present can be convincingly shown to be important inasmuch as neo-Fascist groups and racism are currently in the news. A visit to the Holocaust Museum in Washington, D.C., cannot but give one an almost life-like feel for this chapter in history.

When learning goes beyond registering collections of information, when it engages the learner's mind and feelings, allowing that mind to take the grasp of itself, the power and the joy of teaching and learning are realized.

Dewey believed that any normal student has the potential to share in activities that are intellectual or aesthetic — things we vaguely associate with a snobbish, museum-like idea of "culture." The typical idea of culture or of the humane studies is that they are mere ornaments —

something with which we paint the grim face of real living to impress others or to cover over what truly matters or is too painful to think about. In the democratic vein of Dewey, Richard Mitchell (1987) has made an eloquent case for the thinking ability of students. In *The Gift of Fire* he writes that the great human possibility is that the mind "can take the grasp of itself and its works" (p. 22). While this power is, he acknowledges, "probably unavailable to infants and lunatics, *in the absence of some such special impediment, who can be without it?*" (p. 22, emphasis added).

Let us back up a bit here. These propositions are demanding. No school on earth can meet the spirit of these propositions every day with every student or every teacher. Public schools typically are not organized to give everyone "broad and liberal studies," i.e., studies worthy of a free individual in a democratic society (including, yes, the "vo-tech kids," and the kids in the "low reading group"). Nor are schools typically eager to relate learning to the people, activities, and institutions in the local community as Principle 11 emphasizes. Nor are schools "big" on using subject matter to further inquiry, the thoughtful consideration of ideas, by students or teachers as Principle 12 requires. Yet, since schools do not typically do these things, all the more reason to do them as often and as well as we can. Leavening the boredom and rigidity of schooling in itself is a good thing. By doing so, we give our students and ourselves a hint of what learning and teaching could be. Teacher and students improve their intellectual and social growth in these ways. Why not cultivate ourselves for a more rich and generous life as we cultivate our gardens in the warming sun of summer?

Before we give some positive examples that relate the spirit of these principles to real-life teachers and students, let us insert a brief story about the potential problems flowing from the impersonal nature of technology, an implication of Principle 12. This is from Forrest Williams, then a high school English teacher in Provo, Utah.

Ask the Computer!

Recently, I read a piece by Vito Perrone (1989) in *A Letter to Teachers* in which he was concerned about the learner's inability to assess his or her own performance in a social studies class. My concern went even deeper, however. In Perrone's example, the student responded to the question, "How are you doing in social studies?" with the admission, "I don't know, you'll have to ask my teacher." Yet, the very day I read this I was asked by one of my students, "Mr. Williams, how am I doing in English?" to which I responded, "I don't know; I'll have to check the computer. That's the only way I can be sure how you are doing."

Even as the event unfolded I was shocked! There was I — in my own mind a fine, progressive teacher — a living example, right out in public, of the very problem that Perrone was writing about: *Students* aren't expected to know how they're doing — *teachers* are; or in my case, the *computer* was the source of knowledge!

Now, to some vignettes illustrating the difficulty in bringing about the changes prefigured by the three subject matter principles. That difficulty is suggested in the examples from the Owen J. Roberts School District, Pottstown, Pennsylvania, in which one of the authors is working with teachers and principals in a dialogue-based reform effort. At the time of this writing (early 1994), most of the progressive examples of learning and teaching in this district are add-ons to standard curriculum, teaching, and testing practices, such as those John Goodlad (1984) describes so well in *A Place Called School*. But these add-ons to a standard curriculum demonstrate some feeling by teachers that improvement is needed.

The first example shows how housing for poor families, landscape architecture, and historical preservation link in a volunteer-community project by high school students in the district. The story was printed in the Owen J. Roberts School District bulletin, *The Advocate*, published in December, 1993.

Building Houses and Restoring a Meadow

"Not expecting to be paid for their work [repairing a floor for a needy family] was a new concept for them," said Ms. Tinder. "They learned how important it is to extend a hand and help people out. I think the kids felt good about a hard day of physical work, learning something new and helping a needy family."

The outing was also an opportunity to extend the classroom beyond its walls at the high school, and give the students a chance to put theory into practice, she said. And there are plans for more such expeditions in the future.

In another project the students and their talents in landscaping have caught the eye of Robert W. Montgomery, owner of the region's award-winning nursery and landscape design firm in Chester Springs. The result is a collaboration with Historic Yellow Springs where efforts are underway to recreate the natural ambience that surrounded the historic buildings in the 1920s when the Pennsylvania Academy of Fine Arts conducted their landscaping school there.

One of the major projects at Yellow Springs has been the restoration of a meadow that reflects a turn-of-the-century design with ponds, a stream, spring houses, appropriate planting, and a pathway that winds through it all. This fall the OJR students planted bulbs as part of that project, and next spring they will plant a butterfly garden there.

Mr. Montgomery, said Ms. Tinder, has been a terrific resource for the program. He donated the materials for last year's open house, he conducted the class with the Yellow Springs project, and he hires the students to work in his business.

These experiences lead the students in new directions, and help them solidify choices about their futures, observed Ms. Tinder. They also enhance the reputation of OJR and its students in the community.

The next example from an elementary school in the district extends the idea of community to the rain forests of South America (Principle 11), involves all students in the unit regardless of their ability (Principle 10), and surely helps these third and fourth graders to create "personal meaning," a goal some critics might reject as being too soft, too unmeasurable for a rigorous education (Principle 12). The principal and teachers involved are the source of this narrative.

Tropical Rain Forest Thrives

When the Vincent Elementary PTO invited rain forest expert Bruce Segal for a school-wide assembly about this threatened ecosystem, little did anyone realize what doors this single event would open. In preparation for Segal's visit, third- and fourth-grade teachers decided to incorporate the rain forest into their lessons. And like a wild vine, the rain forest become an integral part of not just science class, but wrapped around reading, writing, art, and social studies, too.

Eventually, the entire student body hopped on the wave of enthusiasm, and what finally emerged in a formerly empty room was a true model of the rain forest in all its splendor.

There is the floor of the forest, the understory, the canopy and the emergent layer. And there are the creatures that call the rain forest home — delightfully colorful and whimsical paper renditions of monkeys, anteaters, toucans and other birds, three-toed sloths, frogs and butterflies. To complete the scene a tape of rain forest sounds plays softly in the background.

This magical room is a vivid example of what can happen when creativity and flexibility merge into an explosion of learning.

"It was total integration — total submersion into the subject," said fourth-grade teacher Nancy Swart. "It engaged every child, it gave a reason for learning, it was totally motivating. However bright they are, they were challenged to the limits."

For example, in language arts class the students read a book about the rain forest and the efforts being made to save it from destruction. They wrote a play based on the book, made their own masks for different roles in the play, and video-taped the production for other classes to use.

They learned about the impact of deforestation on the ecosystem and what its loss means to them. And they learned about the lives of people who live there.

Instead of some far-off remote place where Tarzan swings on the vines, the rain forest became something real and vital in the students' lives, said Swart.

By setting aside the artificial boundaries of time, and integrating the basics into a smooth unit of study that encompassed the 3 R's and much more, simple words on a page were transformed into an exciting chance to learn.

One of the writers of this book had an opportunity to visit this colorful, papier-mâchè rain forest with its butterflies, anteaters, flowers, vines, and trees. To the taped sounds of jungle birds and animals in the background, Angelika, my fourth-grade guide, took me on a tour. Angelika seemed knowledgeable. Explanations and sentences flowed easily: "A lot of animals climb trees to the upper canopy of the rain forest." Pause. She adds thoughtfully, "But not if they don't fly!" As we climbed through vines and stepped across a small stream, she said, "Iguanas run on the top of water. Like on water skis, sort of." We pause to look at a land crab and her babies in the water. "Mike and Josh made those," Angelika notes; her voice suggests pleasure at their accomplishment.

At the end of the tour, Angelika agreed to do a short interview.

Interviewer: Did you like the project?

Angelika: Lots. Kids see their work when they go on tour in the forest. If one kid did it, it would not be as neat.

Interviewer: What did you enjoy most?

Angelika: Writing reports on the forest and papier-mâché. I'm a very organized person. I like to write anything.

Interviewer: What did you learn?

Angelika: Need to protect the rain forest in other countries. They give us oxygen and animals. There are five layers in the rain forest. I will remember some of this when I grow up. Then I want to explore it with my own eyes … see the real thing. This is just a paper rain forest here.

Interviewer: What did your parents think about this unit?

Angelika: They like it a lot. They think it's "extra," though. I think it's part of what we study. All schools should do school-wide projects [this statement refers to rain forest visits by children in other grades]. We did all the work, and we like to show it to people.

Interviewer: Would you like to tell me anything else?

Angelika: The whole thing makes me feel good. I like to answer questions. Feel proud. All of us put a lot of work into it. We shared. Everyone got to have some fun in making things to be part of the rain forest. There is lots to see in here. Someone showed me a sock animal. I didn't see it before. Lots of things you don't notice the first time.

There is no doubt that Angelika is a good student (the teachers were taking no chances with my guide!). Nonetheless, I am certain that if I interviewed every student in the grades who worked on the unit, their responses would show the same joy, personal meaning, and knowledge of something beyond their direct personal experience as Angelika displayed. An activity like this rain forest unit is "all" (to oversimplify in the interests of clarity) that the principles we write about require to make learning and teaching more thoughtful and more personally and socially useful. Try something like this unit with some of your colleagues. It's work, but it's usually work with additional satisfaction.

Teaching Methods

A good school creates learning environments. Although a good school has a general plan for curriculum and may use textbooks (but not to the exclusion of real books from the library), and the teachers in a good school do plan lessons, all of these elements are directed and unified by a few big ideas that help shape a better classroom and school learning environment. Every classroom and school in this country has a learning environment whether the teachers and principals ever think or talk about it or not. The environment is simply there because it is precipitated by what the principal, the teachers, the students, and the community think is important in life and by what all of these actors on the school stage do.

The Owen J. Roberts School District, Pottstown, Pennsylvania, uses four big ideas to guide its reform effort. These design principles arose from discussions with teachers and principals and from a survey and discussion with several hundred parents and citizens in the community. The school board adopted the four principles which we elaborate below.

Four Principles on Which to Build a Better School Environment

- The primary purpose of learning is to cultivate the intelligence and sensitivities of students and teachers.
- Learning is an active process.
- The interaction of students and teachers should be dynamic, inquiring, and vigorous so that increasingly more *independent learning* is desired by students and teachers.
- Flexible patterns of organizing time, subjects, and teachers with students need to be used to support the first three principles.

These principles and a dialogue-based inservice program in which teachers and principals read serious books on learning, educational history, and theory (such as John Dewey's), are beginning to show some concrete results. The account below shows how three teachers who are in the dialogue group at the Warwick School, Owen J. Roberts School District, took action that reflects the spirit of Principles 13 and 14. This account is taken from *The Advocate*, November, 1993, a school district newspaper that goes to people in the community.

Children Make the Connections

During this past summer three fourth-grade teachers at Warwick — Fern Gleason, Darlene Hofmeister, and Nick Zurga — took a hard look at the curriculum and realized that, based on their classroom experiences, there was a better way of teaching it.

So, with a little tinkering here and there, they have modified the current curriculum and turned it into a lively, dynamic learning experience for their students. They accomplished this by rearranging the old lessons into a group of ten unifying themes — themes that serve to tie all the lessons from science, social studies, language arts, and math together into integrated units.

The result is a much more natural learning style, say the teachers, one that is more "hands on" for the students and one that is more flexible for the teachers, freeing them from the constraints of the clock. One lesson flows into the next keeping students' interest at a peak and reinforcing previous lessons.

"The children are making connections," said Ms. Hofmeister. "This makes learning more valuable because it makes more sense. It gives classes more of a focus."

At the beginning of each thematic unit, basic questions about that theme are posed and, by the end of the unit, the students are expected to answer them.

"Systems" was the first theme of this year, and the questions asked required the students to identify the reasons systems are important in everyday life, and what can be learned from them. Their interest was piqued by an introductory brainstorming session in which students identified systems in their lives — everything from stereo systems to septic systems.

Then they got to work. In social studies they learned as part of geography the systems used to design maps and how to read them, and that process carried over into current events. Science focused on weather systems, including air currents, air pressure, moisture in the air, and the water cycle.

Under the language arts banner, their writing skills — another system — were developed. They designed graphic organizers, and read books that enhanced their study of weather systems such as *Night of the Twisters*. In math they learned about temperature, weight, and how to use systems to solve problems.

The knowledge gained from this theme was demonstrated when the children were asked to design a system and then explain through writing and demonstration how it worked — a form of testing known as performance assessment.

Theme units for the rest of the year include challenges, structure and function, balance, diversity, patterns, cycles, changes, interactions, and time and progress. The amount of time spent on each theme varies between two and five weeks, depending on the complexity of the material studied.

Parents are excited by the concept, asking that they be informed of the theme in advance so they can follow through at home. The integrative model can also be adapted by other grades and curricula throughout the district.

Since most of us are traditional teachers trying to make the transition as educational pilots to the more exotic and satisfying "progressive" type of airplane, it is worthwhile to hear the story of Susan Moon, a veteran high school teacher in rural Georgia. Ms. Moon has made the transition from more traditional teaching to Foxfire's holistic approach. Moon's story is in the same vein as that of the three Warwick teachers who are experimenting with larger themes and frameworks to make the content they teach more coherent. Foxfire's eleven core practices[7] provide the framework for Ms. Moon's teaching.

Foxfire's core practices help insure that a supportive classroom and school environment are being created within which the teachers and students do their learning. This meets the criteria of Principle 13. As you read Ms. Moon's story, it becomes clear that this is no drill-for-skill classroom in which subject matter is cut off from students' meaningful experience, as Principle 14 suggests ought not be done. "I like being a facilitator," Ms. Moon writes. "It is pretty exciting when my students become articulate...enough to...be successful in ways that I could not have planned or even imagined." Our experience suggests that if more classrooms offered the rich environment that Susan Moon offers, the number of kids "diagnosed" as learning disabled and ADD (Attention Deficit Disorder) would drop markedly. Ms. Moon's story appeared in the December 1996 issue of *The Active Learner: A Foxfire Journal for Teachers.*

Ms. Moon's English-journalism class is made up of students in grades 9 through 12. This Foxfire class does more than publish a good newspaper — important as that is — but it also is filled with real-life experiences that make a class hum: folklore, oral histories, and mentoring.

Seven Years in a Foxfire Classroom
"Itching" to Re-examine the Core Practices

As I enter my seventh year of implementing the Foxfire approach, I am reminded of the title of a Marilyn Monroe movie, *The Seven Year Itch*. I am "itching" to re-examine the Core Practices as I use them in my classroom.

Please pardon me while I scratch....

Core Practice #1: All the work teachers and students do together must flow from student desire, student concerns.

M-m-m-m! This one feels good!

I can definitely attest to the fact that work in my Back Roads class is infused from the beginning with student choice, design, revision, execution, etc. In fact, the whole first two weeks of each term is spent brainstorming what this year's group wants our class to be.

Even when I tell them that Back Roads does not have to include a product, each class since the first one in the fall of 1990 has chosen to focus on newspaper and magazine production. Storytelling, oral histories, folklore, sharing family traditions, and mentoring projects with the primary and elementary schools are other aspects of the class that have continued to crop up in our brainstorming sessions.

How can I be sure that students' ideas are not overly influenced by me? It helps that during those brainstorming sessions, I am walking around the room with mirrored shades covering my eyes and a wide piece of masking tape covering my mouth, so that I can't influence the students' brainstorming with wide or rolling eyes, excited gasps, or dejected moans.

I have not always agreed with the projects they have come up with, but I have learned from experience to let them work through the projects themselves. Sometimes, I've been pleasantly surprised that a project I felt was completely undoable turned out to be not only doable but profitable as well. One example was our Back Roads Rock-a-Thon, an all-night outside affair that debuted on the coldest night in November, with twenty-odd students rocking in rocking chairs to collect pledge money.

Now the Rock-a-Thon is an annual tradition with former students returning to rock along with us. And you ought to see all the kinds of writing that goes into that project: advertisements, brochures, pledge letters, and much, much more.

Core Practice #2: Therefore, the role of the teacher must be that of collaborator, team leader, and guide rather than boss.

Oooh, yeah! This one's feelin' good, too.

I like being a facilitator, though it isn't always easy. I can see concrete examples of the effects that turning responsibility for learning back on students has on their lives. It is pretty exciting when my students become articulate and powerful enough to take on and be successful in ways that I could not have planned or even imagined.

Still, I admit that it is a struggle each year to get my new students to adjust to my role as a facilitator. Some students who haven't developed the self-discipline required to guide their own learning keep waiting for me to stand over them with a yardstick every minute saying, "Do this! Do that! Not that way! This way!" Sometimes, these students catch fire and become the most active and assertive learners of all. More often than I would like (which is never!) they struggle the entire semester and make a quick exit at the end of the term. It kills me because it doesn't hit every student, and I wish I knew why.

It amazes me that in 1996, there are still students who just can't handle being in a classroom where the teacher asks — yes, even expects — them to take responsibility for their own learning. In the words of several former Back Roads students, "Back Roads is what you make it: It works if you work!"

Core Practice #3: The academic integrity of the work must be absolutely clear.

That's it! Keep scratchin', baby!

I believe this question is answered in my school system every year when my Back Roads juniors' scores are consistently among the highest in our school on the Georgia High School Graduation Test in Writing. Now, I do not take full credit for those scores — they are the sum total of our work together and the good teaching that came before. However, the fact that all my students have scored consistently higher, and that none of them has ever failed the test the first time, does speak pretty loudly.

But then we take our skills seriously. The second week of school, my Back Roads students are introduced to the State Language Arts and Composition objectives. They are also informed that whatever projects and activities they choose must — no excuses accepted — ensure that they meet these objectives. I find that as the year progresses, the objectives are met time and again — and then some.

Core Practice #4: The work is characterized by student action rather than passive receipt of processed information.

Core Practice #5: A constant feature of the process is its emphasis on peer teaching, small group work, and teamwork.

Core Practice #7: There must be an audience beyond the teacher for student work.

and ...

Core Practice #8: As the year progresses, new activities should gracefully spiral out of the old, incorporating lessons learned from past experiences, building on skills and understandings that can now be amplified.

My Back Roads students do not use a textbook to learn about magazine and newspaper production. They learn from studying other newspapers and magazines, and they learn through experience — their own and that of previous students who teach them how to avoid making the same mistakes. Each experienced student has to train another student to take his place.

Taking ownership of the newspaper and magazine also teaches students how to think for themselves. The key word in that last sentence is *think*. The Foxfire approach encourages students to think, to act for themselves, and to accept the responsibility for their thoughts and the consequences of their actions. Sometimes when my students try a new idea for the newspaper or magazine, it bombs! In other words, they fail, but in failing they learn that falling flat on your face means you're still heading forward, and that's what counts. The only true failure in my class is failing to try.

Another case emphasizing just how well these four Core Practices have been "scratched" is my Spanish I class. They asked one day, "Why can't we do something fun like Back Roads is always doing?" This led to a brainstorming session about how they could prove to me that they had learned the language. Several students piped up with, "Why can't we go teach what we learn each week to some students in the primary school?" Thus another project was born — with three groups of Spanish I students traveling across the street to visit three primary school classes (K-2) every other week. There, they taught the little ones what they themselves had learned the previous week.

My students made lesson plans, activities, and evaluation instruments geared to the young learner. Their own evaluation instrument invited the primary school teachers to evaluate their success in implementing the Spanish language with that teacher's class.

What happened as a result of this approach to Spanish? When these same students took Spanish II with me the next year, they wanted to pursue the project again. This time so many primary and elementary teachers had heard of their success, we had twelve partnered groups of students traveling weekly to the primary and elementary classes, serving more than twenty-four teachers in kindergarten through fifth grade.

Now, that's some spiraling, folks!

May I insert an interesting tidbit here? Because my students were doing all this teamwork and peer teaching at the primary and elementary school, we were unable to cover as many chapters in the Spanish text as had the students across the hall. Was I worried? You bet! Would my students be able to compete at the end of the year? Happily, I can answer this with a resounding YES! My students placed second in State Spanish I competition and first in State Spanish II competition.

What does this prove? In my opinion, it proves that living the language, experiencing it, and becoming actively engaged in it provided my students with a learning experience unequaled by a mere textbook approach. Applying the Foxfire approach to Spanish I and II gave my students ownership in the language. I'll never be able to go back to the old way.

Core Practice #6: Connections between the classroom work and surrounding communities and the real world outside the classroom are clear.

and …

Core Practice #9: As teachers, we must acknowledge the worth of aesthetic experience, model that attitude in our interactions with students, and resist the momentum of policies and practices that deprive students of the chance to use their imaginations.

OooEeee! That scratch feels S-O-O-O-O GOOD!

Students in my American Lit, Spanish I and II, and Back Roads classrooms make dozens of connections between the classroom work, their own communities and the world beyond. This happens when students:

- gather and publish "Eldertales"
- travel to the home of Mrs. Bertha Bankston, whose grandmother was a slave in Pike County, in order to capture her essence on paper

- interview local artisan and potter, Jim Webber, to learn about an ancient art form and his link to "brothers in clay"
- strengthen their interviewing skills by inviting speakers to class from the surrounding communities

While watching a potter spin his wheel may be an aesthetic experience all its own, the personal aesthetic experience is best summed up by former student Ryan Wisler, an editorial cartoonist who ended up expressing himself through his artwork. As a newcomer from Oregon, he was thrown into Back Roads because of scheduling problems and wondered what he was doing in a writing class when he "couldn't write." Ryan won the Back Roads award his junior year because, as he realized, "This is the only class I've ever had which played on my strengths and not my weaknesses."

Students who are willing to look can find their own niches in Foxfire classrooms across the nation because Foxfire lends itself to individual aesthetic experiences.

Core Practice #10: Reflection — some conscious, thoughtful time to stand apart from the work itself — is an essential activity that must take place at key points throughout the work.

Core Practice #11: The work must include unstintingly honest, ongoing evaluation for skills and content, and changes in student attitude.

I think that the real itch is over here and that by scratchin' it I've died and gone to heaven!

These two practices have become such an important component of my own classroom that it is hard for me to believe I ever existed without them. On any given day, you might walk into my classroom and find a class meeting in progress. It has usually been called by a student to iron out some problem, discuss a change of plans or simply to get feedback from the rest of the class on an idea she/he has had.

Journals are a weekly part of this class and students don't get any more honest than in their journal entries. They tell me the good, the bad and the ugly about the class, which helps me assess the climate of the classroom.

The finished products — the newspaper, the literary magazine —- allow us to stand back and take a good long look at what we have accomplished. Is it all we had imagined or hoped it would be? Better? Worse? How can we make it better? It is during these periods of reflection and ongoing evaluation that the beauty of the Foxfire teaching approach shines through for me. During those class meetings, reflective brainstorming sessions, and journal reading, I can see wheels of thought turning, ideas forming and problem-solving taking place. It is then that I catch a glimpse of my future, which is in good hands if run by students like these, who have learned to think for themselves and work together to reach a democratic solution to that which ails us.

I guess you could say I'm a Foxfire-convinced teacher. But you need to know, folks, Foxfire is not a panacea or miracle cure for all that ails education and schools today. It does encourage students to take an active role in the learning process by including them in decisions about how — not whether — they learn. And when they catch the fire, they really excel.

Yep, I'd say that my seven-year itch has just been scratched. These eleven Core Practices are not only viable in my classroom, they have become a part of me.

Having had that itch scratched so well, I will lay me down to rest.

What idea (or ideas) — basic principles of learning and teaching — did Susan Moon try to follow in constructing her learning environment? Do you think Ms. Moon needs to buy and use a commercial communications package to raise her students' self-esteem, or use other popular packaged topics, such as "conflict resolution," "thinking skills," "cooperative learning," or "classroom management"? Perhaps she should avail herself of the very latest hot inservice topic — "social skills training" — that invokes rat-maze psychology (Behaviorism) to make kids unthinkingly conform to unnecessarily restrictive school rules, the kinds of rules that support the boring teaching John Goodlad describes so well in *A Place Called School*.

Other principles in *What Every Great Teacher Knows* suggest some of the elements in learning and teaching that must be modified to avoid too direct attention to results. See, for example, Principle 4 on the learner's foresight of ends, and Principle 10 that says broad, general knowledge of social significance should be taught (particularly in the unspecialized world of K to 12 public education).

We make our schools what they are for good or ill by the things we *do*. Our actions, not our words or good intentions, reveal our implicit, generally unexamined *theories* of learning and teaching. "Simple" actions shape the social and intellectual environment — and the emotional environment — in our classrooms. Patti Mortensen, then a third-grade teacher in Provo, Utah, recounts an anecdote about a teacher who probably thought she was doing fine teaching. From this one incident, assuming that this event is true of the teacher's larger pattern of teaching, can you infer some of her deepest beliefs about children, motivation, and learning?

"Losers" Are Made, Not Born

I once substitute-taught for a third-grade teacher. After each and every assignment that was completed, the children would pass their paper to the person behind them for correcting. After the correcting was completed a percentage grade was assigned to each paper and returned to its owner. At this point, the children were then called upon to call out their scores to the teacher for entry into the grade book. I was astonished at the thoughtless disregard for the children's feelings. One student consistently received the lowest score on every assignment and each time he called out his score he was labeled by himself and other students as a "loser."

It is painful to think that there is even one teacher whose *theory* of teaching could lead her to this kind of unnecessary hurtfulness.

PRINCIPLE 15

EVERY GREAT TEACHER SELECTS PROBLEMS
FOR THOUGHTFUL AND MEANINGFUL
ANALYSIS THAT ARE WITHIN THE EXPERIENCE
OF THE LEARNER AT THE START OF THE
LEARNING, RELATED TO THE PROBLEMS OF
ORDINARY LIFE, AND REQUIRE THOUGHT OR
REFLECTION ABOUT THE CONSEQUENCES OF
ACTIONS TAKEN TO SOLVE THE PROBLEM.

Learning begins with a problem of concern to the learner. He or she tries to do something, the content of which is within his or her present experience (read a book, solve $x + 2 = -3$, understand a word, sing a piece of music, sketch a boulder, pass a football, approach the problems of how we can change what we do in this school to cultivate more effectively intelligent actions by teachers, students, and administrators).

If a school faculty (or a subgroup of the faculty) asked itself how their school might be made more thoughtful, Principle 15 would apply explicitly. The question calls for action that is within the present experience of the faculty, that relates to the concerns of their everyday life, and that requires thought.

Educators cannot forget or ignore the following fundamental principle, laid down not only by Dewey, but by other educators: Learning, i.e., growth, cannot "skip over" essential experiences that connect the past to the present. There should be an overlap between the student's previous experience (past learning) and the new experience (present learning or what-is-to-be-learned). Figure 3 presents these ideas visually. Sometimes the "linking experiences" can be adequately supplied by vivid vicarious experience such as a film, field trip, or even a discussion.

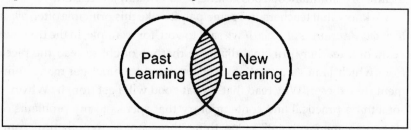

Figure 3. Desirable Education. The shaded area represents past learning (all of one's experiences) overlapping with new learning (what one has not experienced).

The overlap of past and new experiences increases the likelihood that the new learning will "take root" because the new learning is linked to, and becomes an outgrowth of, one's past learning. You as a teacher or principal constantly invoke this principle when it comes to *your own learning*. If we said to you, for example, that we would read and discuss selected chapters from Lawrence Cremin's classic history of education, *The Transformation of the School,* your first comment would be: "Why read *that*? What good will it do [me]? All I want is something concrete to make this curriculum better." If we were moderating your staff development dialogue, the question of "connection" to your past learning should be addressed up front; however, the worth of Cremin's book can only be assessed during and after you encounter it because as you read and discuss it in the dialogue, many of you will make connections that cannot be foreseen prior to the experience with the book.

Learning at any present moment is fed and nurtured by all of one's past learning. New learning enters the mind through the door of memory, past learning. What we have experienced in life — what we have truly learned — influences what we choose to learn in any present time, how deeply we learn it, and how much we like learning what is new. Sometimes when we are pursuing an interest on our own, or working through some complex issue whose core solution seems to lie within shields of granite, we feel as if our mind, feelings, and body have pushed out a bit and led us to occupy a richer life space. Our satisfaction is deep, the air intoxicating. These rare moments of deep intrinsic learning must be an organic development beyond all the learning that preceded them: beyond, yes, but rooted in and growing from all that one had previously learned. This is the psychological continuity of which Dewey speaks and toward which mere "curriculum continuity" — often helpful but still more paper intentions than anything psychologically real — points us. Our teacherly work can only come to life in the theatre of the mind, a theatre of "simultaneous possibilities," as William James said.

We know that teachers and principals invoke this principle often *when their own learning is at issue.* If we said to you, for example, in the first two years of a teacher/principal dialogue that we ought to read the piece from which James's quotation is taken, would we not get many comments like these: "Why read that? What good will I get from it? Why not something practical and contemporary that speaks to my problems of classroom management?" One thing these not-so-hypothetical comments say is this: "*Given all that I have learned to this moment, William James and that stuff doesn't seem to 'fit.' And because it doesn't 'fit' with my past experience, I cannot ingest it and I must, therefore, reject it."*

Your students are very much like you. They try to fit what you are trying to teach them into their past experience. Even rejection speaks to this connection between past and new learning. Although you as a teacher cannot make a tight connection with your students' past learning, even three days a month with 25 or 120 kids, you can try. You can try to build bridges (however small their timbers) that might invite more of your students to surmount the void between what they now know and what they do not know — the new content you are about to teach. The right kind of discussion about how new content might inform some issue of importance (such as the apparent decline in relatively secure, well-paying jobs for white- and blue-collar, middle-class workers) might help forge that essential connection between what you are teaching and the students' past experience. The job future is not very bright for the students in your classes, far less bright than it was, say, for youth beginning work before 1980.

Or you might provide a "linking bridge" between what they know and what you want them to know through a field trip, a speaker, a good film, or maybe even a keen and well-prepared lecture-pep talk — by you. Or you might jump right in and build your linking bridges later. In an English class, for example, the novel to be studied is *Huckleberry Finn*. Although you do the usual things to orient students to the novel and to arouse interest, you might also say, "We are going to spend the first third of our time on this story by addressing this question: How does it help you to see some of your concerns as a teenager in new ways? Is there any connection between Huck's and Jim's concerns and yours? Of course, you might not see any connection between your life and the novel. We'll air these ideas, too." The point here is not the novel as a thing to be learned, but the novel as a vehicle to begin a consideration of their life experience in the context of formal school subject matter.

The arrows in Figure 4 below represent the "experience gap" between what the student knows — his past experience — the minute before you launch your "hot" lesson — his new learning; the new learning has not yet entered his experience stream.

In this diagram, because the new learning does not overlap with past learning, the continuity of experience is broken. Both the student and the teacher may then be forced into the expedients of rote "learning" and

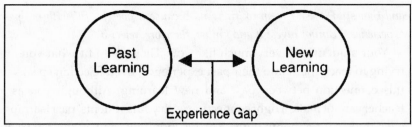

Figure 4. Undesirable Education

drill on unrelated parts of the content such as formulas in mathematics, dates in history, or the textbook definition of inertia in physics.

Two mistakes are to be avoided as we try to apply this principle to our work as teachers. First, we must not expect complete success immediately. "Success" in teaching, as in learning, comes slowly over long periods of time (perhaps two to three years, in the case of complex ideas; perhaps even a lifetime). Learning to meet the spirit of Principle 15 is more difficult, for example, than learning to write the crisp, clear (and often trivial) behavioral objectives advocated by supporters of mastery learning or other ways of teaching that are rooted in a mechanical theory of learning and teaching.

Second, we must not in the early stages of application feel an obligation to try out this principle simultaneously in most of the subjects we teach. Instead, we should try it out in the areas with which we are most comfortable. We should be sensitive, change, adapt, and respect criticism, but not give up with a feeling of failure. The secret consists in steady, persistent efforts to achieve an *environment* where teacher and student will want to participate, communicate, and experience learning. The answer is not a revolution of current practice but rather a gradual evolution and expansion of improved practice.

John Dewey (1944/1916) posed the challenge clearly:

> No one has ever explained why children are so full of questions outside of school ... and the conspicuous absence of display of curiosity about the subject matter of school lessons. Reflection on this striking contrast will throw light upon the question of how far customary school conditions supply a context of experience in which problems naturally suggest themselves. No amount of improvement in personal technique of the instructor will wholly remedy this state of things. There must be more actual material, more stuff, more appliances, and more opportunities for doing things, before the gap can be overcome [p. 155].

We never educate directly, but indirectly by means of the environment [p. 19] ... [in] setting up conditions which stimulate certain visible and tangible ways of acting [p. 34]. In such shared activity, the teacher is a learner, and the learner is, without knowing it, a teacher — and upon the whole, the less consciousness there is, on either side, of either giving or receiving instruction, the better [p. 160].

Some aspects of Piagetian theory support parts of Principle 15, although Piaget was less interested in the "problems of ordinary life" than he was in reasoning in science and mathematics.

- For Piaget and his followers, intelligence is the most necessary instrument of learning; hence, learning of facts and skills is subordinate in importance and emphasis to the thinking aspect, the primary reason for all activities (Furth and Wachs 1974).

- It is not how *fast*, but how *far* we can facilitate the growth of intelligence that is significant (Duckworth 1979).

How does the learner "move" to a higher level of understanding? What Piaget found significant is that understanding *results from a conflict arising in the child's own mind*. It is the child's own *effort* to resolve a conflict that takes him or her to another level (Duckworth 1979; see Principle 2). It occurs when "truth is not given ready-made in the world, nor is an absolute norm imposed on the child" (Furth & Wachs 1974, p. 19).

- Commenting on the use of outside stimuli in learning acceleration experiments, Piaget questioned whether new ideas introduced in this way might not create learner dependency on such outside "pushes" to learn, rather than developing the learner's own initiative in pursuing relationships among ideas (Duckworth 1979). The motivation for learning is intrinsic when children move into situations they find rewarding (Furth and Wachs 1974).

- New knowledge is always based on previous knowledge; new knowledge is a result of the refinement and reintegration of the knowledge one already has (Duckworth 1979).

We argue, with respect to these principles, that Piaget's ideas require an intelligent (less hurried and more democratic) adaptation of many present practices in school administration, curriculum, and teaching.

Take, for example, typical "practical" school procedures. A good case (not an absolute one) can be made that present types of school organization, as well as curriculum and instruction practices, either (1) do not "work" for many kids (be they "bright" or average), or (2) work less well if *educational* criteria are used, rather than the more circular *schooling* criteria: student passivity, facts and skills isolated from problem solving, excessive teacher talk and direction, and little chance for students to generate problems of academic and democratic significance. Educational criteria relate learning to life outside the school and are not limited to tiny, fragmented steps of lessons, or even one-year courses or grades; they contemplate learning that results in understanding something; learning that enhances one's capacity and confidence; learning that is thinking.

It is time that teachers and administrators speak up for the conditions required for better learning. No other source is so powerful and so close to the action. Reflect on one very practical problem — that of trying to teach a great deal of content in an effort to accelerate learning. If we selected learning experiences in a manner consistent with the spirit of Principle 15, think of the changes that might result in the never-ending "content" of social studies, sciences, and English/Language Arts. Adoption of the following provocative idea from Grant Wiggins and exploration of the practices that flow from it would foster intelligent curriculum development: The right curriculum, Wiggins asserts, is the one that "develops in students the habits of mind required for a lifetime of recognizing and exploring one's ignorance" (1989, p. 57).

If social studies is, for example, among the subjects least liked by secondary students, and if the content is not learned, even measured by its own limited criteria, what do we have to lose by more intelligently redefining it?

Our reform agenda for better civic preparation might come from a small-as-yet, but growing, number of educators who propose a *thoughtful* social studies curriculum radically at variance with the "skill and drill" technology so much in evidence these days. For example, Fred Newmann and associates conducted a large-scale examination of classroom discourse in high school social studies classes (1990a, 1990b, 1991). While not disparaging the acquisition of skills (by which Newmann means the "tools for manipulating knowledge" [1990a p. 47]), the researchers note that without a *disposition* to act thoughtfully, learners will tend toward both rote learning and rote application of knowledge. The investigators propose six "dimensions" of teaching and learning to define the thought-ful classroom (adapted from 1992, pp. 68-69):

- A few topics received sustained examination rather than many topics being covered superficially.

- The lesson displayed substantive coherence and continuity.

- Students were given an appropriate amount of time to think, that is, to prepare responses to questions.

- The teacher asked challenging questions and/or structured challenging tasks (given the ability level and preparation of the students).

- The teacher was a model of thoughtfulness.

- Students offered explanations and reasons for their conclusions.

For other examples of both philosophy and curricula of "thoughtful" schools, see Brown 1991; Webb et al. 1996; Wiggins 1989.

Marilyn Prettyman, principal at Longview Elementary School in Murray, Utah, reports a school experience that we would wish for all secondary learners.

Out of the Cocoon

In my senior year at the Idaho Falls High School I spent nine wonderful months with a master teacher. It was as though I had existed the previous eleven years in a cocoon and emerged from her room with the freedom of a butterfly. She took us from the dry farms of Idaho on a marvelous trip around the world and back through time. We debated with the citizens of Athens and Sparta as to the merits of their communities, ruled with Charlemagne, discussed revolution with the Russians and the French, painted with Monet and Picasso, heard music with Beethoven and Mozart, and learned about the dark side of man in World War II. I don't know how she had the time to correct all the reports, maps, and essay tests or the hours it took to plan each lesson for us. I only know that my life was never the same after Miss Neuber's class. Some of the greatest joys of my life come in those moments when my mind reaches and stretches; a feeling I had not known until that year.

We catch the excitement and poetry in Ms. Prettyman's account of her trip around an intellectual world. Notice her images — she emerged from her school cocoon as a butterfly; her "debate with the citizens of Athens and Sparta; she painted with Monet. Surely Ms. Prettyman's vital experience meets the substance of Principle 15. How could something so educationally good be without thought, be beyond her experience? Need we doubt that this class, and Miss Neuber, have become part of the writer's "ordinary experience"?

In *Teacher Efficacy and Quality Schooling*, Lanier and Sedlak offer a precise, strongly-worded critique of teaching and "learning" that does not provide what Principle 15 suggests: "School learning is severed from learning and living outside of school.... The trivialization of valuable knowledge, habits of mind, and skills into school learning has been one of the greatest failures of our efforts to educate effectively" (1989, p. 119).

PRINCIPLE 16

EVERY GREAT TEACHER ALLOWS STUDENTS
TO TRY OUT IDEAS FROM THE CURRICULUM IN
THEIR PRESENT EXPERIENCE BECAUSE,
WITHOUT THIS "TRYING OUT," IDEAS DO NOT
MOVE FROM THE REALM OF THE ABSTRACT OR
"SCHOOL" TO THE STUDENTS'
PERSONAL AND COMMUNITY LIFE.

PRINCIPLE 17

EVERY GREAT TEACHER KNOWS THAT
INDIVIDUALS MUST HAVE AN OPPORTUNITY TO
CONSIDER AND SHAPE GROUP ENDS.
LEARNING ACTIVITIES SHOULD SUPPORT
EDUCATIVE GROUP WORK, SHARED
EXPERIENCE, CONVERSATION, AND
INDIVIDUAL WORK.

One of the best kept secrets in education is the learning power generated when small groups of students discuss and defend ideas, suggest and defend alternatives to solve a problem, or share information and tentative understandings about something worth talking about. Yet teachers rarely use small groups to energize intellectual, social, and moral learning. As studies repeatedly show, most classrooms are taught as a total group with teacher talk dominating 70 percent of the talking time (Cuban 1984; Goodlad 1984). And most of this talk deals with low-level fact recall that demands only short, phrase-like answers. Rarely do students use oral language to "compose" sentences and paragraphs. This avoidance of self-constructed learning fails to arouse interest and inhibits the development of the power to think, analyze, defend, or explain. Principles 16 and 17 offer an antidote to the anti-social work environment of most schools. Small group work within a thematic unit or a project is a practical way for students to set some goals of their own, which should increase student interest and sense of personal responsibility for their actions.

Group work, while it does not automatically do so, can lead to the formation of learning communities — groups of individuals bound by mutual ties of inquiry. Powerful learning forces are generated in such groups. As Piaget (1932) notes, one does not "get" or "receive" an idea or a moral value from the outside. Such things do not come in packages to be given by teachers to their students. Ideas and values can only be *constructed* from *within* the learner. In this construction (note its active rather than passive quality) the learner tries to form relationships with and connections to what he or she already knows.

Social interactions — such as talking in small groups — are essential for this cognitive construction to take place: Exchanges of points of view lead to intellectual, moral, and social learning. Cooperation — individuals operating together to frame and to solve a problem, mutually supportive, yet without losing their individuality — is necessary for intellectual development. Talking about ideas or other sensible things leads to criticism of ideas by others. This suppresses a thoughtless "I am right" attitude because the students have a chance to introduce other content, to counter ideas and questions, to request justifications, and to evaluate the logic of what others say.

Finally, the power of learning in small groups leads to the optimistic view that

> schools remain one of the few institutions that have potential for strengthening America's sense of community [because] they encourage and reward the involvement of both children and adults in matters of mutual interest, in the identification and solution of vital community problems: isolation, poverty, physical deterioration. (Lanier & Sedlak 1989, p. 130)

Thus, something very ordinary like "discussion" turns out to be a worthy intellectual process because it is reflective and interactive. It is not something nicely sequenced in advance, with students routinely jumping the hurdles of textbook questions or workbook exercises. The conversation is more truly intellectual because of the give-and-take of serious talk.

Dewey's contribution to this idea is the notion that all learning is social (learning requires people to interact within a culture and to talk — use language — in social interaction); that learning is active, not passive; that present learning is built on past learning; and that the essence of intellectual activity is the solving of problems of social and personal importance.

Notice that these ideas do not talk alone of "skills," of test scores, of more time in school, of self-esteem or cooperative learning that come in a kit, of time-on-task, of remedial instruction, nor of a dozen other things that occupy the attention of "practical" educators in staff meetings, school board meetings, and quick-fix inservice programs, world without end, as the preacher says.

Constance Kamii has given illustrations of teacher questions that focus small group student talk: What do you think of...? Does everybody agree with...? How many different interpretations of the poem did we have in this group? She also reports (1984) a study by Perret-Clermont that draws this conclusion: When children confront the ideas of other children for as brief a time as 10 minutes, higher levels of reasoning often result. Moreover, the children could transfer this level of reasoning to areas not covered in the experiment. This and other related studies support Piaget's and Dewey's belief in the power of social interaction to affect something as seemingly remote as reasoning.

The following vignette is derived from Kamii (1984)

Sentence Diagramming as a Thoughtful Activity

The very idea that thinking — the development of the cranial super-computer that we call "mind" — can be energized by something as ordinary as thoughtful talk sounds so effete that it demands an earthy classroom example. Let's use a grammar lesson. Certainly, if small group effort is effective in a grammar lesson — given that the subject must rank close behind economics and education in God's list of deadly subjects — teachers can have confidence in the application of the method to other, less lethal, subject matter. Remember, too, that small group work in which students *learn* to become more responsible learners, has been part of good progressive schools since the 1920s.

The point of the lesson is this: By embedding the diagramming of a sentence in a dialogue/small group process, the intellectual and interest level of the lesson was raised a metaphorical 5,000 feet in educational altitude.

A class of 30 sixth-grade students was divided into groups of five students. The teacher gave the groups 20 minutes to diagram the same sentence. One student from each group wrote the diagram of the sentence on the board, thus displaying the work of each group for all to see.

Having set the stage, i.e., created a rich environment for some high-level learning, the teacher then said something like this, "O.K. Explain and defend your diagram." From this point on, the teacher moved to the background, intervening only to facilitate the explain-and-defend lesson. The students got into the discussion by giving well-reasoned arguments in favor of each group's version of the correct sentence diagram. Counter-arguments filled the air. Discussion was intense. After a while, only two of the six diagrams survived the give-and-take of criticism. After recess, the teacher asked if the students wanted to know the correct answer. As some said "Yes" and others said "No," no answer was given. Discussion continued. The class finally agreed on the superiority of one sentence. In sum, a sixth-grade class spent an afternoon on a "grammar" lesson; yet the students did not suffer the ignominy of passive "mind-stuffing," but rather produced a high-energy session of personally significant learning.

This lesson is worth thinking about. What reasons can you give, from your own knowledge and what you have picked up so far in *What Every Great Teacher Knows*, to support the contention that this lesson is superior from the perspective of both practice and theory? Or why is it not superior, if you believe that to be true? (You might want to break into small groups to discuss this question!)

Mr. Larry Dean, a high school teacher at Aspen Elementary, Orem, Utah, tells of a personally significant experience illustrative of the kind of action suggested by Principles 16 and 17.

Interest Up, Scores Up in Social Studies

As I studied [books on thinking], I became uncomfortably certain that my teaching approach of many years was wanting, so I decided to make a change. Beginning with a unit on the Civil War, I pretested both my morning and afternoon 10th-grade core classes on the concepts to be covered. Both classes averaged about 39% on the pretest.

Using my conventional classroom approach, I taught the unit to my morning group of students, relaying the information from the text using my all-too-familiar lecturing approach.

With the afternoon core group, I tried other ideas: I tried to create a classroom setting in which thoughtful learning might occur. Dividing the 30 students into two groups of 15, I asked a student teacher to advise one group and I advised the other. We assigned a project leader from each of the sub-groups. We brought in 40 books (for example, *The Blockade: Runners & Raiders; The Confederate High Tide; Sherman's March to the Sea)* and three video tapes about the war. The project leaders divided their groups into three groups of five students each.

To help with the group effort, the individuals were assigned different tasks, e.g., finding out all they could about several of the great battles of the war. Throughout the activity, we advisors offered advice if asked, leaving full autonomy to both of the original sub-groups. (Some examples of the limited advice that was sought: Advanced vocabulary was explained; suggestions for how to motivate less enthusiastic group members was provided.) After just three weeks of this arrangement, I simply was not prepared for what followed: I have never seen my students so energized and full of enthusiasm. They devoured the information in the books as if they were starving for knowledge nourishment. At the same time, of course, my morning group, learning about the same unit, was acting lethargic as usual.

To satisfy my old habits, we administered the same end-of-unit test to both groups. The morning group scored a class average of 68%. The afternoon group scored a class average of 90%.

It was a bitter pill to swallow: In the guise of efficiency, but in reality for the sake of class control, I had been boring my students to tears for some 12 years.

Mr. Vernon Dunn, a teacher at Bingham High School, near Salt Lake City, tells of his experience in allowing students to take a hand in the conduct of their class as suggested by Principle 17.

Students as Co-Conspirators in Learning

At the beginning of this school year, our high school adopted a new attendance policy. We have implemented a new one about every three years for a long time. I was not really happy with the new one, but did very little about it to start with.

In January I picked up a tape recording of a book on leadership. I wasn't initially thinking of the attendance policy as I listened to the tape, but in the middle of the tape, as he was explaining how employees perform better when they sense ownership in the business and its products, I began to wonder if that might also be true of students in the classroom. I decided to find out. I thought I would begin the third quarter with a new attendance policy that had been devised by the students in class.

As I read and prepared to begin this experiment, I began to feel that if I were to let the students have a say in the attendance, I would be hypocritical if I didn't allow them to voice their concerns about other classroom issues, too. I ended up giving them the assignment to devise an attendance policy, a grading policy and scale, and a curriculum for the remainder of the year.

I told them that I knew that this was a high-risk approach, and that if it were to work, they would have to take it seriously. In order to give them some direction, I explained some principles to them and shared with them the mission statements of the school and the English Department. I also explained to them that their class and individual mission statements had to be in alignment with the departmental and school mission statements if they were to be acceptable and successful.

To get each student involved in the decision-making process, I split each class into groups of four or five students with the assignment to generate written solutions for curriculum, attendance, and grading. After each group had completed its proposals, I put them on the board and moderated the class discussion before conducting a class vote on each proposal.

In each area I provided them with three or four alternatives that I had found could at least serve as springboards for their group discussions. In the area of curriculum, I gave them 12 or 13 books and topics that I was or could be prepared to study with them. They were to pick three or four that could be covered by the end of the year.

The attendance policies (each class devised its own) they established contained two or three key ingredients. First, they felt that any policy that did not reward them for promptness and regular attendance would not motivate them very much. Second, they included methods to recover lost attendance points that were fair to both the teacher and the student. Third, while they steadfastly maintained that attaching any penalty to the grade was unfair, eventually they concluded that nothing else would motivate a student to attend class.

In both 11th-grade college preparation English classes, the grade scale they settled on was the same one that I had been using before — even though five or six other scales had been proposed. In the regular 11th-grade English class the students chose to lower the grade scale 10% from 60% to 50% for a passing grade. True, one scale was proposed by one group that 10% would be a passing grade, but the rest of the class immediately emphasized in loud terms that such a scale would not be in alignment with the established mission statement of the school and the department. I didn't have to say anything.

The long-term effects are not yet evident, but so far attendance in my regular English class has risen about 10 to 15%. While attendance is seldom a problem in the college preparation classes, four or five habitually tardy students have made a concerted effort not only to be on time, but to be the first students in the room, as they remind me almost daily. It is still too early to determine the effect of the overall class grades, but more students are approaching me with genuine concern over what they will miss when they need to be gone for athletic and other school activities.

One thing that might be perceived as a drawback is that it took three to four weeks of class discussion and presentation to arrive at the policies in each class. While that seems to be a lengthy process and much time away from "English" studies,

I was prepared to spend that much time because I knew that this is one process that cannot be rushed. I anticipated that it would not be easy for students who had never before had the opportunity to make democratic decisions for themselves. After going through the process, I do not consider the time wasted in any way. Much more was learned by each member of the class than I had hoped for. One student commented that she had no idea how hard it would be to get 30 people to agree on anything.

A second drawback, and this is a real one, is that now instead of two preparations for three English classes, I must prepare for three that have different curricula, different attendance policies, and different goals as independent classes. I am convinced, however, that all the extra work is more than worth the results gained from giving the students ownership in their classes.

There are several other concerns that keep occurring that tell me that I have not come to the end of the process, nor have I solved all the problems that are attached to this approach, but I am still convinced that this is the right direction to go.

Mrs. Beverly Adair, who then taught at Monticello Elementary School in southeast Utah, tried to involve second graders in real-world problem-solving.

But What Does the Principal Do?

During the 1988–1989, school year my class of second graders held a class meeting each week during which time students identified a problem. We discussed it and considered multiple solutions. During the first meetings, the children had difficulty identifying problems and the discussion was more show and tell than problem solving. However, after several discussions some children began to present problems such as tattling, fighting on the playground, or how to be a good friend. They also discussed questions such as, "Is there a Santa Claus?" "Why do we have school?" and "What does the principal do?"

The children did not always come to a conclusion or find a solution, but they did, from time to time, solve some important problems such as identifying the need for more equipment for use during recess. They also had experience in identifying multiple solutions and working together. I was surprised when, at the end of the year, more than half of the students listed class meetings as their favorite activity.

The more "natural" school activities become, the more students will like them — and learn.

PRINCIPLE 18

EVERY GREAT TEACHER UNDERSTANDS WHERE A SERIES OF LESSONS IS HEADING, SEES THE LOGICAL ORDER OF THE CONTENT, AND TRIES TO RELATE THAT CONTENT TO THE LEARNER'S MORE FLUID, PARTIAL VIEW OF IT.

The following two teachers' tales illustrate the importance of direct experience in students' *and* teachers' learning. In the first tale, a teacher tells how a trolley ride helped students see that not all neighborhoods in their city were marked by buildings with boarded-up windows and broken glass on the streets. Ms. Gail Raznov, then Coordinator of the Mission Excellence program for the Philadelphia Schools, tells how she and parents used the trolley ride to link kids' present and partial experience to a social studies-English unit on understanding the place where they lived — a complex entity we call a city.

A Trolley Ride as Social Studies

Ride the #23 trolley from one end of Philadelphia to another and see the world change every mile or so. That's what an entire school of 180 urban black and white youngsters in grades K-7 did as part of their study of cities. Most had never traveled by public transportation outside of their immediate neighborhood.

We rode the bus to Chestnut Hill and boarded the trolley. Chestnut Hill with its stately mansions and manicured lawns led into quaint storefronts, boutiques, fashionable restaurants. Students' eyes bulged. They asked in disbelief, "Is this Philadelphia?" When I replied that it is, some said, "I want to live here someday." "Do you see any black people around here?" snapped one. "I'll live here if I want," asserted another.

Chestnut Hill gave way to Mount Airy. Trees still abounded, but the difference was perceptible to the students. They noticed that the stores weren't as quaint, houses were closer to each other, and there were black people on the street; people wore jeans, not that preppy look of a few miles back. When the evaluations were tallied the next day, this neighborhood — Mount Airy — rated the highest for the type of area students would choose to live in.

Ludlow scored the lowest. Boarded-up windows and doors, graffiti-scarred walls, abandoned and gutted cars, trash and swirling dirt made them wince. The last stop, in South Philadelphia, featured a tour of the Italian Market and lunch in a restaurant where waiters served and cloth napkins were used. Older students, who had been paired with the younger, reminded them of their table manners. "Please" and "Thank you" were used often, and everyone was on his or her best behavior. It was an eye-opening, consciousness-raising experience.

When the students discussed the trip the next day, some decided to write letters to the mayor, others plotted the trip on a city map. Pictures and stories and poems were generated. Older people reported that they tended to look at things they would normally pass by, such as pocket playgrounds, wall murals, brightly colored signs and the street vendors. They reported that they felt, not unpleasantly, like a kid again and could appreciate things they usually took for granted. Youngsters enjoyed the attention and help, especially in writing their reports, that the olders gave them. There was a flood of questions about the Italian Market from kids who were used to the antiseptic flavor of the supermarket. They were curious about the many blocks of the market they had missed and said they wanted to return with their families. The spice and cheese shops, the poultry and rabbit shops with their redolent odors, stuck in students' memories. This shared experience, with the follow-up activities and conversation, provided a rich base for learning and expression of feelings.

Linking the present experience of the learner to the content is central if a teacher wants to avoid the learning-as-trivial-memorization syndrome. Students *learn* to consider school teaching insignificant when it aims at subject matter divorced from their present lives. Dewey (1944/1916) noted the unfortunate consequence of extensive experience in such classrooms: "Unconsciously, but none the less surely, the student comes to believe in certain 'methods' of learning and ... of teaching which are somehow especially appropriate to the school...." and inappropriate to real life.

Principle 18 may sum up John Dewey's view of teaching, learning, teachers, and kids — if indeed one sentence can point to his views on something so devilishly difficult. One way to restate this principle is to say that the teacher's essential purpose is to create bridges and links between a learner's partial view of, say, language or science, and the more logical, organized view of these subjects held by the adult. If a teacher can slip into the "experience stream" of her students, what is learned will be more interesting and meaningful. This challenging principle is as true for a graduate school professor as it is for an elementary school teacher.

Oh, how easily these words roll off the keys and onto the paper. Too easily. The words are true, we do believe, but they miss ... they miss the learner's experience as she tries this idea in real life — the very thing demanded by Principle 18. That is why we shall introduce you to Tracy, a teacher who is struggling in the choppy seas that separate standard teaching from a Deweyan-progressive kind of teaching. Tracy's story is told with empathy and insight by Melanie W. Chadwick, of West Chester, Pennsylvania. Melanie, a graduate student, struggled herself to write this account as part of a hands-on experience in a supervision course that viewed teaching as art and the observer/supervisor as an art critic. The purpose of the teacher observation was to make the art work of teaching more available to the teacher and to others. Tracy's story is much longer than the other stories we have told. We want you to know Tracy, to see her on stage, to meet some of the actors in her drama, not all of whom act with intelligence, thereby increasing the difficulty for this strong teacher as she tries to become a better, more thoughtful one.

Tracy's struggle, the nearly irresistible pull, for example, of nine years of standard teaching in a parochial school, is the struggle each of us has if we are trying to grow, first, as a human being, second, as a teacher. Our past experience holds both the flowers of what we might become as well as the weeds of what we are leaving behind. And, as Tracy's story leads us to believe, schooling, when it operates as a bureaucratic system, cultivates in unequal measure the weeds and the flowers within the school experience. All of this makes learning to teach in better ways insuperably difficult. We are proud to share with you the story of Tracy, a teacher in transition and under pressure.

What particular insights about you and your own school situation are illuminated by Tracy's story?

Tracy: A Teacher in Transition and Under Pressure

A Few Words of Introduction

I know Palace Park Elementary School from the viewpoint of a long-term visitor. I have been assigned to this primary school (kindergarten through second grade, special education, and special-needs kindergarten) for five years. While I teach in Palace Park I teach for the special school for orthopedically handicapped children. The special school occupies five of the 27 classrooms in Palace Park.

During the 25-year-old life of the school, the beige brick, E-shaped structure has remained the same while the suburban neighborhood has evolved from white-collar to blue-collar. Low-income housing has attracted many black families from the nearby city. Teachers, who have been teaching in the building for years, now commute to work from distant, more spacious developments.

Whatever is now occurring in the building is best understood in contrast to what the school was like when I first saw it. Once yellowing plants in the entrance way are fresh with new green growth. Giant papier-mâché spiders and fantastic spider webs replace dusty cobwebs. The glass show cases previously filled with static uniform displays now contain projects and artwork that spill over to the surrounding wall. Missing fluorescent fixtures have returned, lending lightness and brightness. Real children's work has begun to cover the gray tile walls.

While Houghton-Mifflin still dominates, teachers have tentatively begun to explore the unknown Houghton-Mifflin "Whole Language" series. Teachers go forth in a great deal of uncertainty and doubt, hoping to find a well-charted map for a strange new direction. Quick-credit-accumulating teacher center courses still exist, but the inservice program of choice is the University of Pennsylvania Literacy course, sponsored by the new superintendent.

Other changes are filtering into the school. Slowly, teachers are replacing their two-inch heels with sneakers and flats. Suede and wool straight skirts are giving way to loose washable skirts and slacks. Gone are the daily booming five-minute interruptions over the public address system. Much administrivia is now handled daily in written form. Once the school had a principal who enjoyed making a grand entrance in the cafeteria draped in a red cape and crown. He was the king of the palace; the teachers his "girls." Two years ago a new principal arrived in suit and tie whose presence in the cafeteria fosters order and cleanliness. Professionalism reigns.

Tracy

Tracy strides into school wearing a smile. She never seems to take herself too seriously. One of her favorite subjects for humor is herself. As Tracy passes our jovial "queen-sized" librarian, they exchange friendly jabs about each other's hips. Whenever Tracy is in the midst of a group of teachers, laughs are bound to erupt. Tracy's chuckle clearly chimes over the rest.

This is Tracy's second year of teaching at Palace Park, following a seven-year sabbatical from the profession. After teaching for the local Catholic archdiocese for nine years, Tracy left to explore the business world, "travel, have fun and meet some men." Tracy married a man living with his two adolescent children. Two cherubic baby girls later, Tracy was ready to return to the classroom. She wants to "make school more fun and less severe" than her previous school was. "And I did!"

she proudly says to friends. Bringing fun to her classroom is important to Tracy.

From today's reading lesson Tracy leads the children into a spirited discussion of cheerleading. Boys and girls eagerly raise their hands to share what they know. Tracy indicates the next activity is to produce their own cheer. Tracy scans her teacher manual, puts it aside, and enthusiastically declares, "Let's do it in groups. O.K., everybody, line up." The children eagerly scuffle to line up in front of Tracy. On Tracy's request they begin to count off by fours. Tracy stops the group. "Guys, do you think you could do this in groups of three or four that you choose yourself? You've done it before."

"Yeah!"

"Wow!"

"Sure!"

"O.K., O.K., no more than four in a group and remember everyone needs to be a part of a group. You've got ten minutes to write your cheers then share them with the class. Find a place to work and get started."

The class quickly divides itself. Tracy finds a place for a couple of stragglers. The room is buzzing…. The class is ready in record time. Tracy lets the children know she is impressed with their speed.

The children collect around the rug in front of the room. Tracy sits in her rocking chair, asking each group to perform for the others. She has Jennifer work the lights as the dim room signals a curtain between acts. Self-satisfied smiles abound with the pleasure of their work as the children applaud each other's performances.

Tracy always speaks enthusiastically about her job in Pioneer School District. Last summer she was a participant in a two-day "whole language" workshop and was determined to "give it a try." Her arm shot up at the first faculty meeting this year when the principal asked for a volunteer to use the new Houghton-Mifflin series. Tracy has nothing but positive comments about Palace Park. "This place is great! You can learn so much. The public schools provide so many inservice programs. Not like the parochial schools." She shares with me a book the principal had purchased for each second-grade teacher. The book contains activities a teacher might use instead of traditional worksheets. Tracy likes to experiment with the suggestions the book offers.

As openly as Tracy accepted me in her classroom, she shares her concerns and insecurities about teaching science. Yet Tracy is willing to tackle a lesson on magnets and an exploration of circuits. I have visited Tracy's class several afternoons during her scheduled science time. She tells me how she charmed her husband into spending the previous evening explaining the concept of the magnet activity in a science kit.

In her first year at Palace Park, Tracy had been assigned to a special second grade. The children had been together the year before as a first-grade "readiness class." I recall conversations with Tracy last spring in which she had been given the word to "get the children through" certain second-grade basals. The principal didn't care how she did it, even if it was just to teach to the unit tests. She was feeling overwhelmed. The principal was feeling pressure from central administration to decrease the number of retentions in the building while getting the children "ready" to move on to the upper elementary school.

No "readiness" classes exist in the building this year. Tracy has a heterogeneous second-grade class. However, all Chapter I children have been grouped in two other classrooms. The seven second-grade teachers have attempted to eliminate the typical three reading groups in each classroom. The teachers' goal was to reduce the amount of time the children were doing busy work in their seats and increase the time for reading. To accomplish this the second-grade children change classes for a single 75 minutes of reading each day. The reading groups are determined by ability — the grades the children received in first grade. Tracy was thrilled to be a part of such an

arrangement and to have a "class of kids that could do something." Tracy told me she has "the A-B kids" — the children who
had received A's and B's in reading in first grade. While 75
minutes seems a generous time block, the pressure to "complete" reading in a designated period takes its toll on Tracy and
the children.

As I open the door to Tracy's room, two or three children
wave tentatively and smile. It is reading time. I tiptoe to my usual
seat in the back of the room. A few familiar faces look up at me.
Tracy is slowly pacing between the double rows of desks, the
Houghton-Mifflin teacher's manual held open in her arms. "My
teacher's book says you should be able to read the whole book
by yourself by now. But let's read page 79 together." Some read,
some drone, some play with their fingers and some let their
eyes drift out the window. "O.K. Next paragraph, take turns
reading. Girls, then boys. Girls...." " Girls read. Boys read. Girls
read. Boys read.

I start to play with my fingers. My eyes drift out the window.
A child walking to the bathroom breaks my mental drift. A sign
— BATHROOM — dangles from his arm.

"Justin!! Write your name on the board"! I look about. What
did I miss? The children are no longer reading from their
"anthologies" — collections of stories by well-known authors.
"Let's read the next question in your journal together."

I feel confused. I look about. A booklet of activities and
questions lies open on each child's desk. This is the Houghton-
Mifflin "journal." The children join in choral reading, "How could
you earn enough money to buy a guitar?" Tracy repeats the
question and a few hands go up. Children respond with short
answers. Tracy expands upon each child's ideas. "Now work
on this section by yourself. You must make good sense. You
are in second grade. Give me grown-up answers that let me
know you know the answer." Gazing up at the clock, "You have
five, hmmm, seven minutes to do this part."

Below the clock is a sign:

They may forget
what you said
But they will never forget
how you made them feel!

Tracy walks about the room as the children begin to write. She peers over Robby to see his scratched pencil responses. "What's strung from the neck of the guitar?" Robby looks puzzled. "The neck of the guitar?" Tracy's voice rises as she repeats herself. Robby cocks his head and shrugs his shoulders. "I told you to go back to the story." As Tracy points at the page she asks, "Does this tell you what is strung on the neck of the guitar?" She pauses just a second. Again she asks, "What's strung from the neck of the guitar? Just read it again, Hon." Tracy raises her eyebrows and rolls her eyes in frustration as she looks at me and walks toward another child.

Tracy wanders about the room commenting as she stops at different desks. "You could'a' put down more...."

Near the front of the room Tracy again glances at the clock. Confusing, disjointed directions follow. Tracy calls the class to focus on her. "O.K. kids, we've got lots of work to do today. We've got to catch up. We've spent too long on this story. If you haven't finished take it home for homework. Mark the page number with HW [homework]."

On the board in neat, bold primary print are two columns of words labeled Consonant Clusters.

As Tracy talks the task begins to emerge — underline the consonant cluster. Tracy alternately calls on boys and girls. She adds to the task as each of the first three children attempt to follow her changing directions. By the third child the task has expanded to say the word, underline the consonant cluster and say, "The consonant cluster is _____." She prompts the next two children to restate the complete sentence. By the end of the first column of words a child manages to meet all of Tracy's revised expectations without a prompt.

[Lesson continues]

"We have three minutes left. Quick, who can tell me a word beginning with a consonant cluster?" A few hands go up, a few answers are blurted into the air. Tracy writes. Children tell. Tracy tenders, "Good." "That's right." "Great word, Hon."

As children flow out of the room, one small boy in a coat edges his way in. "Where have you been, honey?" Tracy asks.

"The dentist."

With her arm around his shoulder Tracy quips, "Bet you'd rather have been here." Maybe Tracy would rather have spent the morning at the dentist.

The 75-minute reading period is just one piece of evidence that the staff and administration are struggling with the meaning and understanding of "whole language." Tracy also speaks to me in frustration about all the materials she needs to cover before June, especially the English book. She says the second-grade teachers are weighing the pros and cons of grouping the children for intensive reading for 75 minutes a day. The reading series has so many activities there is not enough time to do all of them. While English is taught as a separate subject, Tracy does not believe she has a good sense of the English skills her students are covering in their separate reading groups. During an inservice-day activity, Tracy illustrates her pull between integrated and traditional language arts pedagogy.

A portion of the inservice day in February was devoted to literacy and whole language. The teachers are sharing activities they and their children enjoyed which supported literacy development. Tracy first shares a page of contractions which could be used for varied flashcard and seat-work activities. She expresses her concerns that the children aren't learning some important material. She thinks the new reading materials and Penn Literacy were too "lah-dee-dah" about grammar and English. "That's the advantage of parochial school. The kids had to memorize this stuff and really learn it." She also shares a book about Harriet Tubman which she used in class integrating vocabulary and writing activities with her February social studies unit for Black History Month.

Today, Tracy introduces me to a new boy, Tommy, who has just arrived in her room. She then directs Robert to tell him about tornadoes. As Robert begins his enthusiastic explanation Tracy pipes up, "No, No, silly! Go get the *Weekly Reader* and read the part to him." Robert complies. He walks over to the counter and returns with the *Weekly Reader.* He reads to Tommy in a halting, flat voice. Tommy glances down and around.

The pressure to cover material also short-circuits Tracy's discussions. This pressure makes thinking virtually impossible and reduces students' self-confidence.

Tracy looks at her teacher manual. The children have just finished an autobiographical story by a famous author and illustrator. In preparation for a follow-up activity they are putting crayons on their desk.

"Are you ready? I'll wait 'til you're ready. I have one minute to explain it. You have five minutes to do this part. We've read a story about Tomi dePoala when he was a child. He wanted to be an artist. What is an artist?"

Children call out, "He paints." "A person that draws." "He uses clay."

Quickly, Tracy defines for the children, "An artist is someone who paints or draws. You take it seriously. You are good at it. You spend a lot of your free time doing it."

Tracy directs the children to read the directions in their books in chorale style.

Although Tracy at times seems to be searching for "right answers," she is willing to change things in her room. She also seems very comfortable with student movement while other activities are going on. Student desk arrangements change every other week or so. When I asked Tracy about new arrangements she replied how she likes to rearrange furniture, but her husband doesn't like her to do it at home, so she does it at school.

Tracy has recently lost her bright smile and positive attitude. The school district may not muster enough support to pass the tax referendum. Tracy, a nontenured teacher, is scheduled to get her pink slip the first week in May.

Tracy has the makings of a risk taker. She feels comfortable with children working in different physical and social arrangements. She is willing to try a new reading series. She is attempting to replace work-sheets with activities that are not neat, prescriptive, and boring. Tracy tackles science although she admits that she may not understand the activities herself. She volunteers to join a few teachers using a new whole-language-basal series. She wants the children to have fun in her classroom.

Tracy is trying to learn and grow. She expresses excitement over the inservice opportunities in the district. She is trying to learn alternative approaches to teaching reading.

We believe Tracy is a teacher under pressure to cover material before the year is over. The message she received from her principal last year lingers. The regrouping of children for reading as a 75-minute subject adds to the pressure. This kind of grouping separates reading from the English content that Tracy feels compelled to cover.

Tracy compartmentalizes subject matter. English, reading, and science have their own scheduled blocks of time. When anything else comes up, science is replaced. The reading series dictates themes. Because of sched-uling and the push to "cover material," even the prescribed themes from the reading series appear lost as potential units within which to integrate some of the content.

Though Tracy is trying the whole language series and has participated in the first Penn Literacy course and a two-day whole language inservice session, she still believes children need to memorize certain material out of context to "learn it." She is struggling to put theory into practice. Reading, writing, and speaking are seen as separate entities. Because of the uniqueness of the new reading program, Tracy follows the teacher's manual like a recipe book. Tracy has had nine years of teaching experi-ence in a very traditional school.

Tracy's style suggests certain beliefs about learning: teaching is telling and learning is remembering. Tracy dominates the discussions she starts. She tells the children much. We rarely observed her encourage the children to search for deeper meanings, encourage thinking, or try to understand thought processes. Does Tracy believe second-graders don't have the mental ability or that children need to be told the "right" answers, or that time is too "valuable" to try alternative approaches? We sometimes think Tracy believes "right" answers come from the teachers, administrators, and textbook publishers.

Unknowingly, the administration hampers Tracy's development. If the administration doesn't understand how and why whole language, Penn Literacy, thematic units, and interesting activities all fit together, how can the administration support Tracy's mindful growth as a teacher? Tracy feels pressured to cover material in breadth, not depth. As a condition for being a pilot teacher for the new reading series, she was asked to make the series her complete reading program. Using any textbook exclusively contradicts the idea of whole language. By supporting regrouping for reading, the administration implicitly supports discrete subject matter knowledge, something that is played out in Tracy's room. A book of activities becomes simply activities and supports the mindset that "this new stuff," this new way of teaching, is just that — a bunch of activities. "It is not enough just to introduce ... games, handwork.... Everything depends upon the way in which they are employed" (Dewey 1944/1916, p. 196).

Tracy has begun her journey in understanding the relationship between children's learning and a dynamic curriculum. In-depth, child-centered discussions and problem solving need to replace short answer and "right answer" sessions. Who is challenging Tracy's assumptions about teaching or learning, or are these the assumptions of her peers and principal? Where are the support systems to encourage Tracy to reflect and develop activities for thoughtful work for children? To make major changes in her pedagogy and curriculum is an overwhelming experience for any teacher without help. Deborah Meier says that making changes in one's teaching practice is like learning "how to drive while changing not only the tire but also the transmission system" (Meier 1995, p. 601). Tracy has come a long way in the two years she has been at Palace Park. We have great confidence in her desire and ability to keep growing. Keep on truckin', Tracy!

Tracy's story helps us see that content can be "fluid" for a teacher in transition to progressive teaching while, at the same time, the content is "fluid" for the teachers' less mature students. Such is the baffling complexity of our enterprise. Deborah Meier's (1995) practical account of teaching in a progressive high school is important reading for teachers who, like Tracy, are trying to travel beyond standard practices.

A FINAL COMMENT

In *What Every Great Teacher Knows* we have provided an opportunity for you — teachers and teachers-to-be — to engage in thoughtful discussions about significant ideas. We see the ideas contained in this book as springboards from which you launch intelligent dialogue, which in turn leads to knowledge, convictions, and practical decisions that affect both adults and pupils in schools. We have tried to be brief in our comments on the principles — provocatively brief, we hope — intending thereby to avoid constraining or coercing your talking and thinking; we have tried to direct your thinking and conversation to humane and intellectual concerns that have always directed intellectual, progressive education.

As we have claimed throughout the book, mind-expanding teaching does not lend itself to prescribing narrow "outcomes" of learning. Rather, it aims at freeing one to sense one's own perplexity and, hence, one's own questions, in order to construct personally and socially significant meaning. Certainly, we do not have in view some precise "learning outcome" that we expect you to "achieve" as a result of working through *What Every Great Teacher Knows*.

On the other hand, our broad aim has been that you would be intellectually and even emotionally engaged with the ideas and stories of *What Every Great Teacher Knows*, and that this, in turn, would lead you to want to talk to colleagues, to engage more formally in a dialogue that requires reading and discussing some classic and contemporary books (Gibboney 1994). The best assurance that a school will become a thoughtful place is that the teachers and principal in the school themselves become more thoughtful.

Notes

[1] Thomas A. Romberg and Thomas P. Carpenter, two top experts in progressive mathematics education, criticize the research on effective teaching by saying this research confuses teaching substance with fancy statistics, that this research is intellectually incoherent, and because this research is guided by no ideas, its empirical findings are circular and not useful. See their article titled "Research on Teaching and Learning Mathematics: Two Disciplines of Scientific Inquiry," in the *Handbook of Research on Teaching, 3rd edition*, Merlin G. Wittrock, ed. (New York: Macmillan, 1986, 865); quoted in Gibboney 1994, pp. 138-140.

[2] The unintended irony in the term "sponge activity" is evidence enough of the plan's machine-like quality.

[3] The report, *A Nation at Risk: The Imperative of Educational Reform* (National Commission on Excellence in Education, 1983), was the first of a series of national reports on education which drew attention to the problem.

[4] The research evidence to show that isolated skills transfer to thinking about the content in the curriculum is not persuasive. A readable argument against this isolation tendency is found in Frank Smith's *to think* [sic] (1990) in which he, echoing Dewey, maintains that thinking is necessarily unitary, not neatly divisible into self-contained compartments, such as remembering, understanding, learning. "Learning is not something that is done separately from thinking.... Inferring, concluding, deciding, and solving problems are inseparable from learning" (p. 42). Smith's point is that the "brain is not doing [a number of] things at once.... It is doing one" (p. 44). All of the categories of thinking are invented by us; they are perspectives on human mental activity, which in fact is a "single, continual, undifferentiated event — the brain at work, going about its own affairs" (p. 44).

[5] Nor do other programs agree with the two under consideration: For example, a video/workbook program from the Association of Supervi-

sion and Curriculum Development (ASCD) proposes that there are precisely 23 "tactics for thinking" (Alexandria, VA: ASCD, n.d.).

[6] Hyde and Bizar (1989) believe that "the reduction of reading, writing, mathematics [and thinking] to overt behaviors that can be considered skills … [is] a tragically mistaken notion" (p. 7). The idea, they claim, has "resulted in many teachers unwittingly destroying the *meaningfulness* for children performing these activities."

[7] For an updated list of Foxfire's core practices, contact Sara Day Hatton, Communications Manager, Foxfire Fund, P.O. Box 541, Mountain City, GA 30562-0541.

Appendix

Eighteen Principles That Every Great Teacher Knows

THINKING AND EXPERIENCE

The principles in this section are intended to help teachers (and principals) explore the understanding of thinking and experience that underlies thoughtful and democratic teaching.

1. Every great teacher makes the cultivation of thinking in a decent and humane environment the primary goal of teaching. (Page 23)

2. Every great teacher values and encourages student questioning because questions encourage student and teacher thought. (Page 31)

3. Every great teacher understands that he/she cannot afford to underestimate what is involved in "knowing something" well. (Page 43)

4. Every great teacher realizes that productive experience results from doing something with foresight, with a purpose in mind, then reflecting on the consequences. (Page 50)

5. Every great teacher recognizes that thinking is not separated from doing something with a purpose in mind; that mind is *in* the doing, not *outside* it. (Page 56)

Teaching Objectives

The principles below apply to the goals for student learning set by administrators, teachers, and students.

6. Every great teacher knows that the learning objectives suggest the kind of environment needed to increase the capacities of the learner. (Page 63)

7. Every great teacher knows that the objectives value both *what* is to be learned and *how* it is to be learned. The quality of learning is critically dependent on *how* the objective is achieved. (Page 66)

8. Every great teacher knows that the immediate classroom objectives are made with larger, overarching aims in mind, that they free the student to attain the larger aims. (Page 72)

9. Every great teacher knows that most teaching objectives ought to make sense to the learner at the time of learning and that future learning is built best on what the student has already learned. (Page 77)

Subject Matter

The following principles pertain to the content, the subject matter, considered here apart from method for clarity.

10. Every great teacher knows that *essential* content is knowledge of general *social* significance that is relevant to all students whatever their abilities or interests. (Page 79)

11. Every great teacher knows that content must be related to the needs of the local and regional community. It is intended to improve the quality of future living for both the community and the individual. Content must illuminate significant social issues. (Page 79)

12. Every great teacher knows that content does not consist exclusively in information or data readily available in books, computers, or other media. Rather, good content is subject matter that assists learners in their inquiry and their attempt to create meaning. (Page 79)

TEACHING METHODS

The principles in this section encourage teachers and principals to consider some generic indicators of quality for professional and thoughtful teaching.

13. Every great teacher recognizes that good methods mean the creation of a total school/classroom environment for learning that cultivates the intelligence and sensitivities of learners, teachers, and administrators. (Page 89)

14. Every great teacher understands that direct attention to results for their own sake through rote learning short-circuits meaningful experience and closes down the growth of intelligence. Neither ends nor means can be hurried if one wishes to provoke thoughtful learning. (Page 89)

15. Every great teacher selects problems for thoughtful and meaningful analysis that are within the experience of the learner at the start of the learning, related to the problems of ordinary life, and require thought or reflection about the consequences of actions taken to solve the problem. (Page 101)

16. Every great teacher allows students to try out ideas from the curriculum in their present experience because, without this "trying out," ideas do not move from the realm of the abstract or "school" to the students' personal and community life. (Page 109)

17. Every great teacher knows that individuals must have an opportunity to consider and shape group ends. Learning activities should support educative group work, shared experience, conversation, and individual work. (Page 109)

18. Every great teacher understands where a series of lessons is heading, sees the logical order of the content, and tries to relate that content to the learner's more fluid, partial view of it. (Page 117)

References

Barth, K. 1990. *Improving schools from within: Teachers, parents, and principals can make a difference.* San Francisco: Jossey-Bass.

Bolton, D. 1994. *The documentation and critique of the dialogue approach to professional development in two schools.* Doctoral dissertation. Philadelphia: University of Pennsylvania.

Brown, R. 1991. *Schools of thought: How the politics of literacy shape thinking in the classroom.* San Francisco: Jossey-Bass.

Bruner, J. 1966. *Toward a theory of instruction.* Cambridge, MA: Harvard University Press.

Calfee, R. August, 1988. *Indicators of literacy.* Publication JNE-04 of the Rand Corporation and the Center for Policy Research in Education. Santa Monica, CA: Rand Corporation.

Callahan, R. 1962. *Education and the cult of efficiency.* Chicago: University of Chicago Press.

Campbell, G. 1989. *Staff development through dialogue: A case study in educational problem solving.* Doctoral dissertation. Philadelphia: University of Pennsylvania.

Cremin, L. 1961. *The transformation of the school: Progressivism in American education 1876-1957.* New York: Knopf.

Cuban, L. 1984. *How teachers taught: Constancy and change in American classrooms, 1890-1980.* New York: Longman.

Dewey, J. 1944/1916. *Democracy and education.* New York: Free Press.

Dewey, J. 1938. *Experience and education.* New York: Macmillan.

Dillon, J. 1988. *Questioning and teaching: A manual of practice.* New York: Teachers College Press.

Duckworth, E. 1979. Either we are too early and they can't learn it or we are too late and they know it already: The dilemma. *Harvard Education Review* 49: 297-312.

Elkind, D. 1970. *Children and adolescents: Interpretative essays on Jean Piaget.* New York: Oxford University Press.

Furth, H., and H. Wachs. 1974. *Thinking goes to school: Piaget's theory in practice.* New York: Oxford University Press.

Gardner, H. 1985. *Frames of mind: The theory of multiple intelligences.* New York: Basic Books.

Gardner, H. 1991. *The unschooled mind: How children think and how schools should teach.* New York: Basic Books.

Gibboney, R. 1994. *The stone trumpet: A story of practical school reform 1960 –1990.* Albany: State University of New York Press.

Goodlad, J. 1984. *A place called school.* New York: McGraw-Hill.

Hillocks, G. 1989. Literary texts in classrooms. In P. Jackson, ed. *From Socrates to software: The teacher as text and the text as teacher.* 89th yearbook of the National Society for the Study of Education, Part I. Chicago: The Society.

Holt, J. 1964. *How children fail.* New York: Delta.

Hyde, A., and M. Bizar. 1989. *Thinking in context: Teaching cognitive processes across the elementary school curriculum.* New York: Longman.

James, W. 1992/1890. Two kinds of knowledge. In *Principles of psychology.* (*Great Books of the Western World,* vol. 53). Chicago: Encyclopedia Britannica.

Kamii, C. 1984. Autonomy: The aim of education envisioned by Piaget. *Phi Delta Kappan* 65(6).

Lanier, J., and M. Sedlak. 1989. Teacher efficacy & quality schooling. In T. Sergiovanni and J. Moore, eds. *Schooling for tomorrow: Directing reforms to issues that count.* Boston: Allyn and Bacon.

Little, J. 1982. Seductive images and organizational realities in professional development. In *Rethinking school improvement: Research, craft, and concept,* edited by A. Lieberman. New York: Teachers College Press.

Meier, Deborah. 1995. *The power of their ideas : Lessons for America from a small school in Harlem.* Boston : Beacon Press.

Mitchell, R. 1987. *The gift of fire.* New York: Simon & Schuster.

National Center on Effective Secondary Schools. Research/technical report. ERIC Document ED 326 465.

Newmann, F. 1990a. Higher order thinking in teaching social studies: A rationale for the assessment of classroom thoughtfulness. *Journal of Curriculum Studies.* 22(1)

Newmann, F. 1990b. Qualities of thoughtful social studies classes: An empirical profile. *Journal of Curriculum Studies* 22(3).

Newmann, F. 1991. Higher order thinking in the teaching of social studies: Connections between theory and practice. In J. Voss, D. Perkins, and J. Segal, eds., *Informal reasoning and education*. Hillsdale NJ: Erlbaum.

Paul, R. 1992. *Critical thinking: What every person needs to survive in a rapidly changing world* (rev. 2nd ed.). Rohnert Park, CA: Foundation for Critical Thinking.

Perkins, D. 1992. *Smart schools: From training memories to educating minds*. New York: Free Press.

Perrone, V. 1989. *Working papers: Reflections on teachers, schools, communities*. New York: Teachers College Press.

Piaget, J. 1932. *The moral development of the child*. New York: Free Press.

Postman, N. 1992. *Technopoly*. New York: Knopf.

Saul, J. 1992. *Voltaire's bastards: The dictatorship of reason in the west*. New York: Free Press.

Sharan, S. 1980. Cooperative learning in small groups: Recent methods and effects on achievement, attitudes, and ethnic relations. *Review of Educational Research* 50: 241-271.

Sizer, T. 1984. *Horace's Compromise: The dilemma of the American high school*. Boston: Houghton-Mifflin.

Slavin, R., S. Sharan, S. Kagan, R. Hertz-Lazarowitz, C. Webb, and R. Schmuck, R. (eds.). 1985. *Learning to cooperate, cooperating to learn*. New York: Plenum.

Smith, F. 1990. *to think*. New York: Teachers College Press.

Thrush, A. 1987. *A. Deweyan analysis of the CoRT and instrumental enrichment thinking skills programs*. Doctoral dissertation. Philadelphia: University of Pennsylvania.

Webb, C., L. Shumway, and W. Shute. 1996. *Local schools of thought: A search for purpose in rural education*. Charleston, WV: ERIC/CRESS.

Wegner, G. 1990. What is history? *Democracy & Education* 4:3.

Welsh, P. 1986. *Tales out of school*. New York: Penguin.

Wiggins, G. 1989. The futility of trying to teach everything of importance. *Educational Leadership* 47(3): 44-59.

Wiggins, G. 1993. *Assessing student performance: Exploring the purpose and limits of testing*. San Francisco: Jossey-Bass.